THE

STRENGTH

OF AN EXACTING PASSION

A STUDY OF **ACTS** 18:18 – 28:31

BIBLE STUDY GUIDE

From the Bible-teaching ministry of

Charles R. Swindoll

INSIGHT FOR LIVING

Charles R. Swindoll is a graduate of Dallas Theological Seminary and has served as senior pastor of the First Evangelical Free Church of Fullerton, California, since 1971. Chuck's radio program, "Insight for Living," began in 1979. In addition to his church and radio ministries, Chuck enjoys writing. He has authored numerous books and booklets on a variety of subjects.

Based on the outlines and transcripts of Chuck's sermons, the study guide text is co-authored by Bryce Klabunde, a graduate of Biola University and Dallas Theological Seminary. He also wrote the Living Insights sections.

Editor in Chief:
Cynthia Swindoll

Coauthor of Text:
Bryce Klabunde

Assistant Editor:
Wendy Peterson

Copy Editors:
Deborah Gibbs
Cheryl Gilmore
Glenda Schlahta

Designer:
Gary Lett

Publishing System Specialist:
Bob Haskins

Director, Communications Division:
Deedee Snyder

Manager, Creative Services:
Alene Cooper

Project Supervisor:
Susan Nelson

Print Production Manager:
John Norton

Printer:
Sinclair Printing Company

Unless otherwise identified, all Scripture references are from the New American Standard Bible, © The Lockman Foundation 1960, 1962, 1963, 1968, 1971, 1972, 1973, 1975, 1977. Used by permission. The other translation cited is the Amplified Bible.

An effort has been made to locate sources and obtain permission where necessary for the quotations used in this book. In the event of any unintentional omission, a modification will gladly be incorporated in future printings.

ISBN 0-8499-8437-8
Printed in the United States of America.

COVER DESIGN: Jerry Ford
COVER PHOTOGRAPH: SuperStock, Inc.

CONTENTS

*This message was not a part of the original series but is compatible with it.

INTRODUCTION

We're on the homestretch of our study in the book of Acts. In this third volume, we will learn of Paul's passion to go to Rome and to appear before Emperor Nero that he might boldly testify of the claims of Jesus Christ. As the title of the guide indicates, Paul's is an *exacting* passion. Nothing—absolutely nothing—will deter the Apostle of grace from his stated purpose. He *is* going to Rome!

A wonderful part of this final leg of our trip through Acts is the opportunity to read of Paul's defense of the gospel. Time after time in different settings and before various authorities, the man speaks openly of his faith. What a model! God still honors such courage.

My hope, as always, is that we will not only learn to think our way through the scenes of this ancient record but, equally important, to apply the truths we uncover to our world today. To help make that happen, let's continue to look for practical ways to model the life of determined faith. What is *your* passion? What are you convinced God would have *you* accomplish? What is *your* "Rome"? May this concluding study in Acts set your heart ablaze in your commitment to Christ as Lord.

Chuck Swindoll

PUTTING TRUTH INTO ACTION

K nowledge apart from application falls short of God's desire for His children. He wants us to apply what we learn so that we will change and grow. This study guide was prepared with these goals in mind. As you go through the following pages, we hope your desire to discover biblical truth will grow as your understanding of God's Word increases, and that you will be encouraged to apply what you've learned.

To assist you in your study, we've included a section called ♦ **Living Insights** at the end of each lesson. These exercises will challenge you to study further and to think of specific ways to put your discoveries into action.

On occasion a lesson is followed by a ➤ **Digging Deeper** section, which gives you additional information and resources to probe further into some issues raised in that lesson.

There are many ways to use this guide—in personal devotions, group studies, discussions with friends and family, and Sunday school classes. And, of course, it's an ideal study aid when you're listening to its corresponding "Insight for Living" radio series.

To benefit most from this study guide, we would encourage you to consider it a spiritual journal. That's why we've included space in the **Living Insights** for recording your thoughts and discoveries. We hope you'll return to those sections often for review and encouragement as you continue to grow in your walk with Christ.

Bryce Klabunde

Bryce Klabunde
Coauthor of Text
Author of Living Insights

THE STRENGTH

OF AN EXACTING PASSION

A STUDY OF **ACTS** 18:18 – 28:31

ACTS: THE SPREADING FLAME

Writer: Dr. Luke
Theme: The growth of the early church
Key Verse: Acts 1:8
Major People: Peter and Paul
Central Locations: Jerusalem and Antioch
Prediction Fulfilled: "I will build my church. . . ." (Matt. 16:18)

A Book of Origins:
- Coming of the Holy Spirit
- Beginning of the church and the gifts of the Spirit
- Apostolic authority
- Outbreak of persecution/martyrdom
- World missions
- Grace instead of Law

	The Church Established at Jerusalem*	The Church Scattered to Judea and Samaria*	The Church Extended to "Remotest Part"*
	The church is . . . . . . born . . . tested . . . purified . . . strengthened	The gospel is . . . . . . spreading . . . multiplying . . . changing lives . . . breaking traditions	The witness is . . . . . . extended . . . received and rejected . . . unifying Jews and Gentiles
Chapter Numbers	A.D. 30 1 7	8 12	13 28 A.D. 60
Leaders	The Apostle Peter		The Apostle Paul
Emphasis	Mainly Jews	Mixing Jews and Gentiles	Mainly Gentiles
Time	2 years	13 years	15 years
Scope	City Evangelism	Home Missions	Foreign Missions

© 1977 Charles R. Swindoll. All rights reserved.
*Main headings adapted from Irving L. Jensen, *Acts: An Independent Study* (Chicago, Ill.: Moody Press, 1968), p. 52.

Chapter 1

DISCIPLESHIP ON DISPLAY

Acts 18:18–21, 24–28

The book of Acts is like a symphonic masterpiece. With the opening notes, the major theme—evangelism—soars through Jesus' words:

> "You shall be My witnesses both in Jerusalem, and in all Judea and Samaria, and even to the remotest part of the earth." (1:8b)

"Be my witnesses . . ." The melody steadily builds, at first through a few believers in Jerusalem, who fill the city with the music of the gospel (chaps. 1–7). The second movement spotlights specific musicians, like Philip, Peter, and Saul, as they carry the refrain throughout Judea and Samaria (chaps. 8–12). Then the third movement swells to a full crescendo, as Saul, now called Paul, trumpets the gospel throughout the world, from Jerusalem to Rome (chaps. 13–28).

And, as with any great musical masterpiece, the major theme is supported by subthemes. As we come to Acts 18, we can detect one of these countermelodies if we listen closely. From a few back-row musicians comes the sweet and subtle strain of evangelism's counterpoint—discipleship.

Discipleship Explained

In order to follow discipleship's melodic line, we must first acquaint ourselves with its structure. So let's consider Paul's words on discipleship to his friend Timothy.

Scripturally Stated

> You therefore, my son, be strong in the grace that is in Christ Jesus. And the things which you

1

have heard from me in the presence of many witnesses, these entrust to faithful men, who will be able to teach others also. (2 Tim. 2:1–2)

Paul discipled his spiritual son Timothy by training him to have the kind of character necessary to carry out the Christian life. Rather than merely soaking up all of Paul's teaching, though, Timothy was to train "faithful men," who, in turn, would train others.

What "things" would Paul have shared with Timothy to "entrust" to others? Probably such treasures as the objective truths of Scripture, the well-defined doctrines of the faith, and the character-developing principles of a balanced life. These were not meant to stay locked in a vault but be invested in others.

Historically Illustrated

Actually, discipleship can be traced further back to Jesus' ministry. He determined that His closest followers would also reproduce His teaching in others.

And He went up to the mountain and summoned those whom He Himself wanted, and they came to Him. And He appointed twelve, that they might be with Him, and that He might send them out to preach, and to have authority to cast out the demons. (Mark 3:13–15)

Bringing these men close to Him, Jesus poured His life into them so that when He was gone they would be able to preach to others with power and authority. He wanted to equip them to follow His example and bring others into the kingdom by making disciples. In fact, He would later command them: "Go therefore and make disciples of all the nations" (Matt. 28:19a).

And that was precisely what Paul was doing with Timothy—and with a certain husband and wife named Aquila and Priscilla, who lived in Corinth.

Discipleship Modeled

We don't usually think of Paul as a personal discipler. More likely, we picture him exploring new frontiers for Christ, preaching to great crowds, then moving on. But his life often intoned the intimate theme of discipleship. Let's listen to it as we examine his relationship with Aquila and Priscilla.

Paul in Corinth

Paul arrived in Corinth alone and financially strapped. But with a little searching,

> he found a certain Jew named Aquila, a native of Pontus, having recently come from Italy with his wife Priscilla, because Claudius had commanded all the Jews to leave Rome. He came to them, and because he was of the same trade, he stayed with them and they were working; for by trade they were tent-makers. (Acts 18:2–3)

His first step in discipling this couple was to *associate with them very closely.* He initiated a friendship, worked with them to make tents, and even lived with them. Then, after he had developed a relationship, *he trained them in spiritual matters.* This training included formal times in the synagogue as well as casual times in their home (vv. 4, 11). Whether standing behind a pulpit or lounging by a warm fire, Paul spoke about Christ. His teaching wasn't cloaked in rhetoric; it was clothed in real life, and they eagerly embraced it.

Paul's final discipling step was to *multiply himself through them.* This is implied in his actions when it was time to leave Corinth.

> [He] took leave of the brethren and put out to sea for Syria, and with him were Priscilla and Aquila. . . . And they came to Ephesus, and he left them there. Now he himself entered the synagogue and reasoned with the Jews. And when they asked him to stay for a longer time, he did not consent, but taking leave of them and saying, "I will return to you again if God wills," he set sail from Ephesus. (vv. 18b–21)

After taking Aquila and Priscilla with him to Ephesus, Paul decided to end his second missionary journey by letting them minister there while he went home to Antioch by way of Caesarea and Jerusalem (vv. 22–23). The Ephesians had wanted Paul to stay, but his response was, "You have Aquila and Priscilla. They can do just as good a job as I could." He had multiplied his effectiveness by pouring his life into this couple, who could then carry on the work without him.

But the discipleship subtheme in this passage does not conclude here. A new player picks up the refrain on the next page of the score.

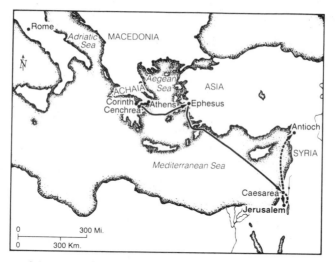

Ministry in Ephesus and End of the Second Journey[1]

Aquila and Priscilla in Ephesus

Aquila and Priscilla were busy establishing the new ministry, when

> a certain Jew named Apollos, an Alexandrian by birth, an eloquent man, came to Ephesus; and he was mighty in the Scriptures. This man had been instructed in the way of the Lord; and being fervent in spirit, he was speaking and teaching accurately the things concerning Jesus, being acquainted only with the baptism of John; and he began to speak out boldly in the synagogue. (vv. 24–26a)

Aquila and Priscilla were immediately impressed by this young man. He was from Alexandria—a university town with a great library and a worldwide reputation for learning. He was "eloquent," or *logios* in Greek, which means he was a gifted speaker and deep thinker.[2]

1. Maps © 1986, 1988 are taken from the *Life Application Bible* © 1988, 1989, 1990, 1991 by Tyndale House Publishers, Inc., Wheaton, IL 60189. Used by permission. All rights reserved. *Life Application* is a trademark of Tyndale House Publishers, Inc.

2. *Logios* "can mean either a man of words (like one 'wordy,' verbose) or a man of ideas, since *logos* was used either for reason or speech." Archibald Thomas Robertson, *Word Pictures in the New Testament* (Grand Rapids, Mich.: Baker Book House, 1930), vol. 3, p. 306.

In addition, he was well versed in the Old Testament Scriptures as well as some of the teachings about Christ. Most significantly, he had a heart on fire. For "fervent in spirit" literally means "'boiling over in his spirit,' that is, full of enthusiasm."[3]

So Aquila and Priscilla listened to him closely, screening all he said through the doctrinal grid Paul had given them. They nodded their heads as Apollos spoke of Jesus—His Messiahship, His deity, and His teaching.

But then the eloquent Alexandrian stopped.

He was "acquainted only with the baptism of John." He did not understand the full orb of the gospel of grace completed with Jesus' crucifixion and resurrection. Neither did he know about the baptism of the Holy Spirit at Pentecost. The Spirit's powerful presence in the believer's life was a foreign concept to him. As accurate as his teaching was about Christ, it was still incomplete and needed attention. Apollos needed to be discipled.

So without embarrassing him, Aquila and Priscilla tactfully reached out to teach this diamond-in-the-rough Christian leader.

> They took him aside and explained to him the way
> of God more accurately. (v. 26b)

Once he grasped the complete truth, there was no holding him back. "He wanted to go across to Achaia" and preach there also (v. 27a). He had his own goals and style of ministry. And rather than squelching him, Aquila and Priscilla, along with the rest of the church, "encouraged him and wrote to the disciples to welcome him" (v. 27a).

As in all positive discipling relationships, there is a time to let go. Discipling is training . . . but it is also releasing the person so that the discipled one can train others. That is what Apollos set out to do when he set sail for Achaia.

Apollos in Achaia

> When he had arrived, he helped greatly those who
> had believed through grace; for he powerfully refuted
> the Jews in public, demonstrating by the Scriptures
> that Jesus was the Christ. (vv. 27b–28)

---

3. Fritz Rienecker, A Linguistic Key to the Greek New Testament, ed. Cleon L. Rogers (Grand Rapids, Mich.: Zondervan Publishing House, Regency Reference Library, 1980), p. 311.

Months earlier, Paul had instructed Aquila and Priscilla; then they had passed their learning on to Apollos; now he voiced the same message to those back in Achaia where Paul had started! Through the discipleship process, the gospel had come full circle, and many more were learning about Jesus Christ.

All this demonstrates the truth we examined in 2 Timothy 2:2. The following chart shows the parallel between Paul's command in that verse and how he himself lived it first.

The Process of Discipleship Illustrated

And the [instructions] which you have heard from me . . .
transmit and entrust (as a deposit) to reliable and faithful men who will be
competent and qualified to teach others also. (2 Tim. 2:2, AMPLIFIED)

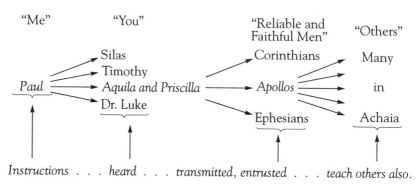

By discipling others, Paul was able to expand his evangelistic ministry in ways unforeseen even by him. In our lives, who knows whom we might be able to reach through the discipleship process?

Discipleship Applied

In this passage, Luke used supporting players instead of first-string instrumentalists to illustrate some prominent principles.

First, *the best relay of truth is discipleship.* In a discipling relationship, we can know one another inside and out. And the better we know one another, the more we learn how to solve real-life problems. Instead of displaying a "perfect" Christian standard no one can reach, discipleship keeps the truth at eye level, making it understandable and accessible.

Second, *the best time to start discipling is now.* Just listening to sermons on Sunday can never substitute for the spiritual charge that occurs in a discipling relationship. Getting close to another person means you'll be taking risks, but they will be worth it when you sense the wonder of the multiplication process—the sense of satisfaction that God has used you to change one person, who changed another, who changed another, who changed another . . .

Living Insights STUDY ONE

Here we are in the first chapter of a study guide, and already we are issuing you a challenge: start making disciples today. Are you ready to try?

If you are not presently involved in a discipling relationship, what barriers have kept you from entering one?

_____

_____

Sometimes we think, "How could I help anyone else in their Christian life? I'm having enough trouble as it is." Take comfort. The best disciplers aren't perfect Christians. Just be caring and authentic . . . and take some initiative.

Begin by imagining your neighborhood, church, or workplace as if it were Corinth. Like Paul, you have just arrived. You want to start your ministry here by discipling someone, but who? Look for someone like Aquila and Priscilla—someone with a background similar to yours, with similar likes and dislikes. Someone with whom you can work well, and someone who is interested in following the Lord.

Who is your Aquila or Priscilla?

_____

How can you associate more closely with this person? How can you build companionship and vulnerability before the training begins?

_____

_____

When it is time to begin training, don't be intimidated. Start simply—read a book of the Bible together, maybe the gospel of Mark. Or work through a study guide together.[4] As you work with this person, keep in mind Walter Henrichsen's advice:

- Remember he belongs to God.
- He must know that you believe in him and that you have confidence in him.
- Do not allow him to become dependent upon you.
- Allow him the freedom to fail.
- Teach him how to evaluate men.
- Seek to instill confidence.[5]

When the person you're discipling has demonstrated the ability to train someone else, your job is through. Now you can begin again with someone new. In its simplest form, that's discipleship. So, are you willing to try?

 *Living Insights*   STUDY TWO

Our most eager and probably most overlooked disciples are our children. Whether you are a parent, grandparent, aunt, uncle, or friend, the children in your life look to you as a model. Have you ever considered discipling them?

How would looking at the children in your life as disciples change your perspective toward them? What would be different about the time you spend with them?

_____

_____

_____

_____

4. You can request an Insight for Living catalog by writing to Post Office Box 69000, Anaheim, California 92817-0900. Your local Christian bookstore should also have a wide selection of study guides available.

5. Excerpted from Walter A. Henrichsen's *Disciples Are Made—Not Born* (Wheaton, Ill.: Scripture Press Publications, Victor Books, 1974), pp. 109–10.

The young ones around you watch closely and copy what they see. How could you use this natural tendency as a discipling tool?

_____

_____

Children are teachable and hungry disciples, but you can't train them using adult techniques. Creativity is the key. To help you explore the ways you can teach spiritual values to children, we've compiled a brief list of resources. Select one or two that are appropriate to their age level, and start discipling them today.

Parenting by Discipleship

Capehart, Jody. *Cherishing and Challenging Your Children.* Wheaton, Ill.: Scripture Press Publications, Victor Books, 1991.

Kincaid, Jorie. *The Power of Modeling.* Colorado Springs, Colo.: NavPress, 1989.

McDowell, Josh. *How to Help Your Child Say "No" to Sexual Pressure.* Waco, Tex.: Word Books Publisher, 1987.

Discipling Ideas

Barclift, Stephen T. *The Beginner's Devotional.* Sisters, Oreg.: Questar Publishers, 1991.

Cooley, Vivien. *Time for Snails and Painting Whales.* Chicago, Ill.: Moody Press, 1987.

Lewis, Paul. *40 Ways to Teach Your Child Values.* Wheaton, Ill.: Tyndale House Publishers, Living Books, 1985.

Merrill, Dean and Grace. *Together at Home: One Hundred Proven Activities to Nurture Your Children's Faith.* Pomona, Calif.: Focus on the Family Publishers, 1988. Distributed by Word Publishing.

Veerman, David R., et al. *101 Questions Children Ask about God.* Wheaton, Ill.: Tyndale House Publishers, 1992.

Williford, Carolyn. *Devotions for Families That Can't Sit Still.* Wheaton, Ill.: Scripture Press Publications, Victor Books, 1990.

Chapter 2

THE MAGNIFICENCE
OF INSIGNIFICANCE

Acts 18:18–23; 19:1, 7

"Image is everything," says the young tennis star in the television commercial as he lowers his sunglasses and winks into the camera. His clothes, his hair, his two-day-old beard are the epitome of contemporary style. He has what the world values most—status, influence, and power.

In a sense, his message is accurate. To be great in our world, image *is* everything. If military generals didn't shine their brass and wear their stars, who would salute them? If politicians didn't arrive in limousines, who would listen to their speeches? If corporate presidents didn't fly first class, who would call them successful? In every realm, greatness seems to require an image of authority and power.

Except in one realm—the family of God.

Jesus explained this exception one day when a certain woman came to Him with a request for her two sons—a request that betrayed the sons' secret ambition for authority according to the world's standard of greatness.

Christ's View of Authority

While Jesus was on His way to Jerusalem, James and John's mother came to Him with a request.

> "Command that in Your kingdom these two sons of mine may sit, one on Your right and one on Your left." (Matt. 20:21b)

In a parallel passage in Mark 10:35–40, we learn that James and John came to Jesus with the same request themselves; so it's probably safe to assume that all three came together. They seem to have figured that Jesus would soon be establishing His kingdom on earth, and Mama wanted to ensure a good position in the new order for her boys. In their way of thinking, sitting next to the King would guarantee them greatness. So the three of them boldly approached the Lord with their request. However, the rest of the disciples bristled at their boldness—because, unfortunately, they wanted power in the kingdom too. As a result, "the ten became indignant with the two brothers" (Matt. 20:24).

What a disheartening scene for Jesus. For more than three years He had been teaching them the value of selfless living. The course was over, graduation was near, and now His prize students were bickering about who was top dog! So, Jesus

> called them to Himself, and said, "You know that the rulers of the Gentiles lord it over them, and their great men exercise authority over them. It is not so among you, but whoever wishes to become great among you shall be your servant, and whoever wishes to be first among you shall be your slave; just as the Son of Man did not come to be served, but to serve, and to give His life a ransom for many." (vv. 25–28)

While the world says, "You've gotta be number one," Jesus says, "In my eyes, greatness is measured by servanthood."

If we desire true greatness, then, we must become servants. But what do servants look like? We need a model.

Paul's Model of Humility

A good example of a person with a servant's heart is Paul. Particularly at the close of his second missionary journey, we can observe his humble attitude in action.

By this time, Christianity's influence had grown beyond Asia to key metropolitan areas of the world. This must have been satisfying to Paul as he left Europe to return to Ephesus, Antioch, and eventually home. And it must have been exciting for believers along the way, who had heard that the gifted Apostle might soon be coming their way! "Want to get a ministry going?" they probably said, "Plug into Paul!" However, despite the notoriety, Paul demonstrated four qualities of greatness in God's eyes, four qualities of a servant.

Private Integrity: A Vow

The first quality is hidden in a brief and seemingly inconsequential detail in Luke's account. He tells us that after Paul had left Corinth for Ephesus with Aquila and Priscilla, he stopped "in Cenchrea and had his hair cut, for he was keeping a vow" (Acts 18:18b). Why would he mention Paul's visit to a small-town barbershop?

11

This haircut represented the fulfillment of a vow Paul had made to the Lord and provides us a rare glimpse into his spiritual life. John Stott explains the nature of Paul's vow:

> The reference to his hair makes it almost certain that it was a Nazirite vow [Num. 6:1–21], which involved abstinence from drinking wine and from cutting one's hair for a period, at the end of which the hair was first cut and then burned, along with other sacrifices, as a symbol of self-offering to God.[1]

In his vow, we see a private integrity that became the spiritual seedbed of Paul's servant heart. Beneath the surface, his godliness was enriching his ministry with quiet, hidden power. And it was also enabling him to remain humble—a particularly difficult response in the midst of success and public acclaim.

Public Popularity: A Refusal

More acclaim met Paul when he arrived in Ephesus with Aquila and Priscilla and started teaching.

> He himself entered the synagogue and reasoned with the Jews. And . . . they asked him to stay for a longer time. (Acts 18:19b–20a)

Wanting a well-known spiritual powerhouse to launch their church, the Ephesians asked Paul to stay. They may have even pleaded with him, saying, "Paul, you're the greatest! People love your teaching, and with you at the helm, this church will go places. You're our man! Please stay."

But "he did not consent" (v. 20b). His no was simple and certain. Confident that Aquila and Priscilla could do a good job without him, he wanted to step out of the way and let their efforts flourish. His servant's heart did not want his popularity to overshadow them.[2]

As a result, their ministry did flourish. They stayed behind and discipled Apollos, who would later travel to Corinth and water the seed of the gospel there (see 1 Cor. 3:4–7). So the work in Ephesus grew, the work in Corinth grew, and Paul wasn't even around!

---

1. John Stott, *The Spirit, the Church, and the World: The Message of Acts* (Downers Grove, Ill.: InterVarsity Press, 1990), pp. 300–301.

2. Compare Paul's attitude with the disciples' response in Mark 9:38 to someone else exorcizing demons in Jesus' name, and note Jesus' comments in verses 39–41.

True servants like Paul don't allow the siren song of fame to convince them of their indispensability. They realize that they are just one among many people who make up a team and who need one another's encouragement. They are willing to reduce their own impact to lift up someone else's. Competitiveness and jealousy have no place in the heart of a servant. Neither is there room for isolationism, as we'll see when we read on.

Voluntary Accountability: A Need

Having promised the people, "I will return to you again if God wills" (Acts 18:21), Paul set sail from Ephesus alone. But as soon as he

> landed at Caesarea, he went up and greeted the church, and went down to Antioch. And having spent some time there, he departed and passed successively through the Galatian region and Phrygia, strengthening all the disciples. (vv. 22–23)

Being a servant, he thrived on relationships, not applause. Instead of organizing flashy engagements for his third missionary journey, he operated side by side with people. He stayed in touch with those who needed him and voluntarily remained accountable to them.

Paul Takes a Third Journey[3]

This is not always a natural tendency for celebrities. Many isolate themselves from people rather than serving them. Fame has a way of revealing their true self-seeking attitude, as the proverb says:

> The crucible is for silver and the furnace for gold,
> And a man is tested by the praise accorded him.
> (Prov. 27:21)

3. Maps © 1986, 1988 are taken from the *Life Application Bible* © 1988, 1989, 1990, 1991 by Tyndale House Publishers, Inc., Wheaton, IL 60189. Used by permission. All rights reserved. *Life Application* is a trademark of Tyndale House Publishers, Inc.

In Paul's crucible, the sparks of praise exposed humility and a genuine concern for individuals. And when he finally arrived back in Ephesus, those servant qualities shone through once again.

Mutual Ministry: A Service

> Paul having passed through the upper country came to Ephesus, and found some disciples. . . . And there were in all about twelve men. (Acts 19:1b, 7)

When Paul returned to Ephesus, he didn't ride into town expecting to immediately take the reins from Aquila and Priscilla. Rather, he supported their ministry by sidling up to just a few disciples and focusing his efforts on them.

In the next chapter, we'll discover more about the nature of his work with these men. What we notice here is that Paul avoided the crowds and the glory, wanting instead to labor alongside the other leaders in a mutual ministry. Paul was not showy or slick, putting himself on a pedestal. Instead, he was like an unobtrusive support column, always there holding others up.

Our Personal Responsibility

Christ's teaching and Paul's example portray a kind of greatness rare in our world. We have a responsibility in our churches to be modern models of this greatness by serving one another. However, servanthood is not easy. It helps to have some guidelines to follow—perhaps these three that we can glean from our study.

First, *resist the temptation to adopt the world's view of greatness.* The church is not a corporation with a CEO, aspiring junior executives, and union laborers. It is a family in which no one person has more value than another, in which meeting needs is more important than growth charts, programs, and image. Ultimately, our only measure for success is the question, Are we serving one another in love?

Second, *we must keep the whole body in focus, not just a small part of it.* Pastors don't make a church great—servants do. Yet we don't seem to believe this, as Howard Snyder observes.

> We depend on our structures and our superstars. And we *know* the system *works*—just look what the superstars are doing in their superchurches! We have the statistics and the buildings and the budgets to prove it.

There is only one problem.

There are not enough superstars to go around. Thousands of churches, but only hundreds of super-stars.

. . . The church of Jesus Christ cannot run on superstars, and God never intended that it should. . . . God does not promise the church an affluence of superstars. But he does promise to provide all necessary leadership through the gifts of the Spirit (Eph. 4:1–16).[4]

The whole body serving one another with their God-given gifts—that is God's ideal for the church.

Third, *emphasize the significance of being a servant*. If we're honest, Christ's message that "the last shall be first" cuts across our grain. How can being last help us be first? It makes sense when we understand the significance of servanthood to God.

To Him, servanthood is not the insecure gesture of digging our toes in the dirt and saying, "Aw, shucks. I'm just a servant. You can step on me if you like." Neither is it a humble-sounding form of spiritual pride or a manipulative martyr complex. Genuine servant-hood is confident love in action—the kind of love that sent Jesus from heaven to a manger and from a manger to a bloodstained cross.

It's what being a follower of Christ is all about.

Living Insights

In a blink, the devil can turn something good like servanthood into something repulsive: slavery. As a result, we resist serving one another, because no one wants to be a slave . . . whipped, taken advantage of, powerless.

The irony is that unless we become servants, we *are* slaves—slaves to pride, greed, and all kinds of dictatorlike sins.

A man in the New Testament who illustrates this irony is Zac-cheus. Take a moment to read his story in Luke 19:1–10.

As the chief tax-gatherer, Zaccheus was the head of a govern-ment-sanctioned Mafia that fleeced the public by collecting inflated

4. Howard A. Snyder, *The Problem of Wineskins: Church Structure in a Technological Age* (Downers Grove, Ill.: Inter-Varsity Press, 1975), pp. 83–84.

taxes and keeping the profit. He was the boss, with power, riches, and success.

Although the Scriptures don't specifically say, why do you suppose he so desperately wanted to see Jesus? What was it about Jesus that may have sparked his interest?

_____

_____

Why do you think he was delighted when Jesus said, "Today I must stay at your house" (v. 5b)?

_____

_____

What was it about the people's grumblings in verse 7 that caused him to suddenly stop and make a vow (v. 8)?

_____

_____

How did pledging to financially serve the poor and return any defrauded money break his bonds of slavery to sin and result in his salvation (vv. 8–10)?

_____

_____

As you reflect on your own life, would you say that you have lately been acting more like a servant or a success-image slave? In what ways?

_____

_____

In what specific ways can you break the bonds of your slavery to self and experience the freedom of servanthood—today?

_____

_____

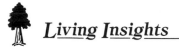

Living Insights

The devil can do another sleight-of-hand trick with servant-hood. If we're not watching closely, he can turn it into something self-serving: performance.

One man who avoided this deception was Oswald Chambers. A model of servanthood, he once said, "Christian service is not our work; loyalty to Jesus is our work."[5] In other words, we can build houses for the poor, visit the sick, or comfort the grieving, but if we do so without an inner, driving loyalty to Jesus, we are performing and not serving.

Lately, what has motivated you in serving others? How do you know when you have or have not had pure motives in your serving?

_____

_____

_____

What can help you serve more and perform less? Consider Paul's attitude in 1 Corinthians 4:1–5. How well does your attitude match up with his?

_____

_____

_____

So much joy is available to you in serving Christ; don't let Satan trick you into serving yourself! It's one of his favorite illusions.

---

5. *Oswald Chambers: The Best from All His Books*, comp. and ed. Harry Verploegh (Nashville, Tenn.: Thomas Nelson Publishers, Oliver-Nelson Books, 1987), p. 319.

Chapter 3

ARE TONGUES AND PROPHECY FOR TODAY?

Acts 19:1–7

As we embark on this stretch of our journey through Acts, we'll come to the top of a ridge overlooking some difficult territory—the regions of tongues and prophecy.

One of the reasons the terrain ahead can get treacherous is because of the differing perspectives people bring to spiritual gifts in general. Charismatics view all the gifts, including tongues and prophecy, as being active and available to the church today.[1] Non-charismatics, on the other hand, say that God now offers the church only some of the gifts—excluding, among others, tongues and prophecy.

With these different points of view can come extremism, which can lead us to stumbling over stereotypes, dropping down onto prejudices, then finally hurtling onto the rocks of divisiveness. So we must proceed carefully here and determine to keep on the path of God's Word, lest we lose our way in the underbrush of opinion and feelings. We must also equip ourselves for the journey with the accoutrements of love: acceptance, humility, and respect.

With these thoughts tucked into our backpacks, let's gingerly take our first step in exploring this terrain.

What Do the Terms Mean?

The gift of tongues is *the supernatural ability to (1) speak in a language other than the one in which an individual is trained or (2) speak in an ecstatic language known to no one.*[2] On the Day of Pentecost,

---

1. The word *charismatic* comes from the Greek word *charisma*, which means "gift of grace." Today the term is associated with those who promote the expression of the gifts of tongues, prophecy, healing, and miracles. These four abilities are sometimes called the sign gifts, because they are viewed as signs of God's endorsement of His messengers and their messages.

2. By "ecstatic," we mean "inarticulate and enthusiastic prayer, praise and thanksgiving in the Spirit." *The New International Dictionary of New Testament Theology*, gen. ed. Colin Brown (Grand Rapids, Mich.: Zondervan Publishing House, Regency Reference Library, 1978), vol. 3, p. 1080. This does not mean that those who had this gift were unable to control it. See the study guide *He Gave Gifts*, coauthored by Bryce Klabunde, from the Bible-teaching ministry of Charles R. Swindoll (Anaheim, Calif.: Insight for Living, 1992), pp. 76–77.

the Holy Spirit empowered the believers in the Upper Room to do the former. As a result, they were able to explain the gospel to the visitors in Jerusalem using a variety of languages and dialects they had never before spoken (Acts 2:1–11).

The latter definition seems to apply to certain believers in Corinth because of specific requirements Paul needed to make for them:

> If anyone speaks in a tongue, it should be by two or at the most three, and each in turn, and let one interpret; but if there is no interpreter, let him keep silent in the church; and let him speak to himself and to God. (1 Cor. 14:27–28)

Such regulations were unnecessary at Pentecost, as was the need for an interpreter. Therefore, we can infer that this was a different kind of tongues.

What was the purpose of this gift? From these passages, and from the general theme of 1 Corinthians 14, we can determine two purposes: evangelism and edification. Speaking in tongues was God's miraculous way of communicating the truth of Christ and building up His church.

Another equally impressive but vastly different gift is prophecy—*the supernatural ability to receive a special revelation from God and to speak that revelation without error*. Prophets spoke God's latest word to people—an ability that was necessary during the days when the New Testament had not yet been completed.[3] In that period, the doctrines about Christ that we take for granted were just being formed. Can you imagine an era with no gospels or epistles to read and grow by?

Let's examine that period of time a little more closely.

When Did the Phenomena Occur?

The expression of tongues and prophecy occurred during the thirty years between Jesus' ascension (Acts 1) and Paul's first Roman imprisonment (Acts 28). This was a time of great historical transition, when the new covenant was being established over the old.

For example, at the beginning of Acts, believers worshiped in

---

3. Luke identifies several of the early church's prophets and prophetesses: Agabus and his companions (Acts 11:27–28), the prophets and teachers in Antioch (13:1), Judas and Silas (15:32), and Philip's daughters (21:8–9).

the synagogue on the Jewish Sabbath, Saturday. Toward the end, they were meeting in house churches on the first day of the week, Sunday (20:7–8). At the beginning, Christian doctrine was in the minds of only a few; by the end, the apostles had started to distribute Christian thought in their writings. At the beginning, only Jews were trusting Christ; but by the end, Gentiles were the majority.

New ways of worshiping, new teaching, new attitudes toward outsiders—these were the kinds of changes Christ was instituting through the new covenant. Acts, therefore, is a book about decades of transition. It represents a state of flux. So we must be careful about getting all of our doctrinal foundations from this book because we may be trying to set in cement something that God hadn't fully formed yet.

The first few verses of Acts 19 are a good case in point. From Luke's opening words, "and it came about," we can tell that what follows, which we'll be looking into on the following pages, was more of a happenstance than a planned movement. Luke isn't even exactly sure how many people were involved—"in all about twelve men"—a smallish group by any standard. And, more significantly, this brief episode is never mentioned again in the rest of Scripture; Paul never uses it to establish a norm or standard of practice for the church.

So, at the risk of being repetitive, we must say again: evaluate the Scripture's context carefully before basing your doctrine on it.

How Did It Transpire?

Now that we have defined our terms and their surroundings, let's forge ahead in Acts 19 to see what exactly transpired between Paul and these twelve men.

Having departed Antioch and visited the churches in Asia (18:22b–23), the Apostle arrives at Ephesus, the beginning of his third missionary journey.

Place and People

In this metropolitan city on the west coast of Asia, Paul discovers some twelve disciples of John the Baptist (19:1b, 3, and 7).[4]

---

4. Although Luke calls them disciples in the account, this doesn't necessarily mean they are Christians. The word *disciple* simply means learner or follower. It can even refer to those who are curious about Christ but not committed to Him, like the disciples who abandoned Jesus (John 6:66).

A. T. Robertson describes them as

> floating followers of the Baptist who drifted into Ephesus and whom Paul found. Some of John's disciples clung to him till his death (John 3:22–25; Luke 7:19; Matt. 14:12). Some of them left Palestine without the further knowledge of Jesus that came after [Jesus'] death and some did not even know that.[5]

Apparently, as Paul quickly ascertained, these men were of the latter sort.

Question and Answer

As he spoke with them, he noticed a few holes in their cup of Christian doctrine. They may have believed that Jesus was the Messiah—John had pointed them to that truth—but were they Christians? Were they trusting His atoning sacrifice on the cross to cover their sins? Were they experiencing new life in Christ as a result of His resurrection? Did they know of His ascension, of His constant intercession on behalf of those who are His own?

To find out, Paul asks them a crucial question: "Did you receive the Holy Spirit when you believed?" (19:2a; compare Rom. 8:9b). And they answer honestly, "No, we have not even heard whether there is a Holy Spirit" (Acts 19:2b). With a discerning question, Paul immediately probes further to find out exactly what they do believe in:

> "Into what then were you baptized?" And they said, "Into John's baptism." (v. 3)

John and Jesus

In the desert, John had preached,

> "Repent, for the kingdom of heaven is at hand. . . . Make ready the way of the Lord." (Matt. 3:2, 3b)

His message had impacted these men, and they had believed it and repented—they may even have seen Jesus. But after John died (14:1–12), they apparently left Palestine and knew nothing of Jesus' death, resurrection, and promise of the Holy Spirit.

5. Archibald Thomas Robertson, *Word Pictures in the New Testament* (Nashville, Tenn.: Broadman Press, 1930), vol. 3, p. 311.

So Paul fills in the missing information right away:

> "John baptized with the baptism of repentance, telling the people to believe in Him who was coming after him, that is, in Jesus." (Acts 19:4)

Belief and Baptism

With hearts wide open, they accept the truth about Jesus and express their new faith by being baptized

> in the name of the Lord Jesus. And when Paul had laid his hands upon them, the Holy Spirit came on them, and they began speaking with tongues and prophesying. (vv. 5b–6)

Paul's laying on of hands was not a requirement for the Holy Spirit to come upon them, for Cornelius received the Spirit without the laying on of hands (10:44–45). Rather, it showed Paul's endorsement of them and their welcome into the body of Christ. For additional confirmation and evidence of their salvation, they spoke in tongues and prophesied. This proved beyond a doubt that they were Christians.

However, it also opens up a can full of questions for us. Should their salvation experience be a model for ours? Should we expect to receive the gift of tongues and prophecy along with the gift of the Holy Spirit? How important should this incident be in formulating our Christian doctrine?

Why Is It Important?

To answer the above questions, we must begin with a premise: everything we do in belief or in behavior must be based on Scripture. No amount of sincere feelings can take the place of biblical facts.

Why emphasize this? So that we can have a sure measure to discern the truth when presented with people's claims and beliefs. For example, some churches have three cardinal doctrines concerning tongues and prophecy: (1) *Subsequence*, the belief that after receiving Christ there is a second work of grace—an infilling of and empowerment by the Holy Spirit. (2) *Evidence*, proof of having received Christ—through tongues and prophecy. And (3) *seeking*, a waiting for and pleading with God for that evidence of salvation.

But is that what happened to these men in Acts 19? They believed, were baptized, received the Holy Spirit, spoke in tongues, and prophesied in *rapid* order. There was no waiting or seeking, and the evidence of tongues and prophecy was an assurance that they were linked to the same body as those believers at Pentecost. "In other words," says John Stott, "they experienced a mini-Pentecost. Better, Pentecost caught up on them."[6]

We do not need an Acts 19 experience in order to fill any spiritual void in our lives. We can know God's fullness of power without speaking in tongues or prophesying, for He has already "blessed us with every spiritual blessing in the heavenly places in Christ" (Eph. 1:3b).

What about *Today?*

As we move past this passage in Acts and its steep, challenging issues, one of the greatest insights we can take with us is the wisdom to separate the essentials from the incidentals. In our passage today, it was not the receiving of the Holy Spirit that was essential but the basis of salvation—faith in Jesus Christ alone.

It is essential that our salvation is based on the correct foundation, Jesus Christ. Our church membership, our experiences, our desires to please God are not the basis of our faith. Only Christ is. Also, *it is essential that whatever evidences follow salvation be just as much from God.* Our experiences must result from the Lord's work in our lives. If they are His work, they will be supported by His Word, and He will receive the glory.

 **L_iving I_nsights**

The gift of speaking in tongues has been called "the biggest Christian friendship and oneness buster of the century."[7] Why do you think this gift has wreaked such havoc in the body of Christ?

_____

_____

6. John Stott, *The Spirit, the Church, and the World: The Message of Acts* (Downers Grove, Ill.: InterVarsity Press, 1990), pp. 304–5. God was granting John's disciples their own Pentecost experience, just like the ones He gave to the other groups in Acts—the Jews (2:1–11), the Samaritans (8:14–17), and the Gentiles (10:44–48).

7. George Mallone, *Those Controversial Gifts* (Downers Grove, Ill.: InterVarsity Press, 1983), p. 79.

Look again at your answer to that question. Are you doing some finger pointing in your response? Is the problem the *other* person's fault? Do you detect any bitterness in your words?

If so, reflect on Jesus' words in Matthew 7:1–5. Imagine that He is referring to those who judge others for speaking or not speaking in tongues. By what standard do you measure the spirituality of those on the other side of this issue?

Christ says, "By your standard of measure, it will be measured to you" (v. 2b). That's a sobering thought! That's why it is vital to remove any "logs" from your own eye. The following is a list of possible logs. Mark the ones that you've noticed floating around in your eye.

❏ Twisting Scripture to say what I want it to say.

❏ Accepting people's interpretations without verifying it in the Bible for myself.

❏ Not willing to listen to anyone else's insights.

❏ Categorizing those on the other side as all the same.

❏ Refusing to associate with those on the other side.

❏ Gossiping about those on the other side.

❏ Only reading books which reflect my point of view.

Do you see any others? Write them down.

What do you plan to do to stop the issue of speaking in tongues from being "the biggest Christian friendship and oneness buster" of the *next* century?

_____

_____

_____

_____

_____

 *Living Insights*

Have you ever heard anyone preface a comment with, "The Lord told me . . ."? How can you know whether the Lord actually revealed His message to that person? Or maybe you have even felt that the Lord was telling you something. How can you be sure?

One test is found in Deuteronomy 18:21–22. In Old Testament days, how could the people differentiate between true and false prophets?

_____

_____

The Bereans had another way of determining whether the Lord actually was speaking through a person. What was their method (see Acts 17:10–11)?

_____

_____

God communicates to us through a variety of means—the counsel of others, circumstances, personal impressions. But the most usual and reliable channel is His Word. So be a noble Berean and examine the Scriptures daily.

Chapter 4

GOD'S EXTRAORDINARY POWER

Acts 19:8–20

Consider God's power. With a wave of His hand, He can carve out a canyon, shift the tides, or fling a million stars into place. He can topple a mountain or slice an atom, rearrange the seasons or redesign a snowflake.

None of these, though, can match the most mysterious and wondrous display of His power: *change.* He can take a life chained in the deepest darkness and set it free to flourish in the liberty of light . . . take a heart that was nearly dead with despair and revive it with the strong beat of hope.

A young woman, teetering dangerously close to suicide's dark edge, experienced such power of God one Sunday in church. She later wrote to the pastor:

> I came and sat in your church huddled in despair and hope. The despair deep and devastating, the hope illusory. I agonized over every word and every aspect of my life's story trying to make it credible to myself, giving it the kind of interpretation that will keep alive a hope.
>
> I just wanted someone to know that when I left, I was different, [a] new person. All this week I have been slowly discarding the illusions, challenging some assumptions . . . trying out new thoughts and ways of behaving . . . based not only on what I heard Sunday, but on the stuff in the Bible. I am delighted in the possibility of being remade. I came to your church with a revolver and a suicide note. From now on I will come only with my Bible. The circumstances aren't vastly, horribly, wonderfully changed . . . but I am.[1]

Her story could have come straight out of Acts—which is,

---

1. From a personal letter written to Charles R. Swindoll.

26

essentially, a record of one changed life after another. Peter the deserter became Peter the evangelist. James the traditionalist Jew became James the welcomer of Gentiles. And Saul the church destroyer became Paul the church planter. Throughout Acts, God changed people and brought new life to them and, through them, to entire continents.

The continent where we'll be standing with the apostle Paul is Asia Minor, in the dark and desperate city of Ephesus. And here we'll consider God's power to change—a power no less extraordinary now than it was in the first century.

Some Initial Observations

As we enter this ancient, yet ageless city, we would do well to keep in mind three basic characteristics of human nature which will help prepare us for the people and situations we'll be meeting.

About People in General

First, *we are sinful and stubborn*. Rooted in the depravity that came with Adam at the Fall, this condition is often modified through humanism, but never really changed. Second, *we are attracted by and attached to things*. The root of this condition is our natural insecurity, which tries to find relief in the mirage of materialism. And third, *we are ignorant and unaware of the enemy*. Curiosity often opens our ears to the siren song of supernaturalism. But, the song is deceptive; it leads us to destruction instead of to the life-giving change we'd hoped to find.

Each of these characteristics will unfold in our Scripture passage, as will God's extraordinary power to overcome them—changing the Ephesians' lives from the inside out.

About Ephesus in Particular

In many respects, the Ephesian people reflected their city's personality. Known as the Treasure House of Asia,[2] Ephesus was the region's capital and was situated at the mouth of the Cayster River. In its heydey, it was the guardian of Asia's hinterland, with ships from all around the world docking at its seaport.

This setting contributed to the opportunistic, business-minded

---

2. See William Barclay, *The Acts of the Apostles*, rev. ed., The Daily Study Bible Series (Philadelphia, Pa.: Westminster Press, 1976), p. 140.

side of the Ephesians, but what shaped the people even more was the city's pagan religious character. As John Stott elaborates,

> Ephesus was famed as "the guardian of the temple of Artemis" (19:35). In classical mythology Artemis (whom the Romans called Diana) was a virgin huntress, but in Ephesus she had somehow become identified with an Asian fertility goddess. Ephesus guarded with immense pride both her grotesque many-breasted image . . . and the magnificent temple which housed it. This structure had more than one hundred Ionic pillars, each sixty feet high, and supporting a white marble roof. Being four times the size of the Parthenon in Athens, and adorned by many beautiful paintings and sculptures, it was regarded as one of the seven wonders of the world.[3]

Superstitious worship degenerated into unrestrained immorality and debased pagan rituals. And into this sinful, materialistic bastion of Satan came the apostle Paul, preaching the simple but powerful gospel of Christ.

Surface Signs of Success

In many ways, Paul's ministry prospered here, and we see several signs of that success in Acts 19. First, the work had *strong and capable leadership*. Paul could speak as few others in his day. Though intelligent and scholarly, he was still able to explain God's glorious truths in shirt-sleeve Greek. So, when he taught in the synagogue during his first three months there, he spoke effectively and "boldly . . . , reasoning and persuading them about the kingdom of God" (v. 8b).

The second sign of success was *vast popularity*. After leaving the synagogue, Paul spent the next two years expanding his work "so that all who lived in Asia heard the word of the Lord, both Jews and Greeks" (v. 10).

Another sign was the presence of *divine miracles*. To validate and support His Apostle's efforts, "God was performing extraordinary miracles by the hands of Paul" (v. 11). With irrefutable evidence, God made the power of His presence known.

---

3. John Stott, *The Spirit, the Church, and the World: The Message of Acts* (Downers Grove, Ill.: InterVarsity Press, 1990), p. 294.

Finally, *the rapid growth* of the movement signified success as well. As Luke records, "the word of the Lord was growing mightily and prevailing" (v. 20).

Paul's efforts gleamed with success, but let's not think that they were won without hardship. Beneath the shiny exterior of rapid growth and amazing miracles, the ministry was encountering incredible struggles and pressures. The sources of these pressures were people whose unredeemed nature was like ours—sinful, attracted to things, and ignorant of the enemy. They tried to restrict the work of the Lord, and that made the ministry's growth costly.

Grueling Grind of Growth

As time went by, the excitement of expansion became a grueling grind because of three opposing forces: fleshly resistance, demonic involvement, and worldly attachment. Yet Paul and his coworkers responded in a way that released God's extraordinary power to change lives anyway, as we'll see in the following verses.

Fleshly Resistance

Luke writes that Paul taught in the synagogue only three months (v. 8). Why not longer? Verse 9 gives us the reason.

> But when some were becoming hardened and disobedient, speaking evil of the Way before the multitude, he withdrew from them and took away the disciples, reasoning daily in the school of Tyrannus.

During those three months, Paul perceived angry walls building up around the hearts of the people in the synagogue.[4] When in their disbelief they began openly blasting the gospel, Paul reacted wisely—he left.

Taking his group of followers, he began teaching instead in the lecture hall of Tyrannus. An ancient manuscript of Acts specifies that here Paul taught "from the fifth hour to the tenth."[5] In other words, from 11 A.M. to 4 P.M., while Ephesian businesses closed for a mid-day break. "But Paul," John Stott tells us, "did not sleep in the daytime."

---

4. The imperfect tenses of the words *hardened* and *disobedient* imply a continuing process. The more Paul taught, the more resistant they became.

5. As quoted by Stott in *Spirit, Church, and World*, p. 313.

Until 11 a.m. he would work at his tentmaking and Tyrannus would give his lectures. At 11, however, Tyrannus would go to rest, . . . and Paul would exchange leather-work for lecture-work, continuing for five hours, and stopping only at 4 p.m. when work was resumed in the city. Assuming that the apostle kept one day in seven for worship and rest, he will have given a daily five-hour lecture six days a week for two years, which makes 3,120 hours of gospel argument![6]

Leaving the synagogue was the best move Paul could have made. There he had faced nothing but fleshly resistance, but at the school of Tyrannus, hearts were softer and opportunities to preach were greater. And the Lord honored his move, empowering him with miraculous abilities.

Handkerchiefs or aprons were even carried from his body to the sick, and the diseases left them and the evil spirits went out. (v. 12)

These aprons and handkerchiefs—literally sweatbands—were things Paul used as he worked at his tentmaking. They were ordinary items, not like the sacred charms or prayer cloths used by some today who promise similar healings. Yet God adopted them as His tools to change lives.

Demonic Involvement

Seeing the miracles and coveting the Apostle's influence was another group who attempted to restrict the gospel.

Some of the Jewish exorcists, who went from place to place, attempted to name over those who had the evil spirits the name of the Lord Jesus, saying, "I adjure you by Jesus whom Paul preaches." And seven sons of one Sceva, a Jewish chief priest, were doing this. (vv. 13–14)

These sons of Sceva weren't from God; they just wanted a piece of the action. They bypassed the Lord's authentic power and imitated Paul's methods, with their eyes firmly focused on the popularity

6. Stott, Spirit, Church, and World, pp. 313–14.

and money that could come from working miracles. But even the demons knew a cheap imitation when they saw one—or seven of them, in this case.

> The evil spirit answered and said to them, "I recognize Jesus, and I know about Paul, but who are you?" And the man, in whom was the evil spirit, leaped on them and subdued all of them and overpowered them, so that they fled out of that house naked and wounded. And this became known to all, both Jews and Greeks, who lived in Ephesus; and fear fell upon them all and the name of the Lord Jesus was being magnified. (vv. 15–17)

Wanting to overshadow Paul and show off their own power, these men ended up demonstrating Christ's power instead. Word of what had happened spread, and the people were amazed that even the demons respected Jesus. Once again, God overcame human restrictions and opened the door to victory.

Worldly Attachment

That victory became a turning point in the lives of many of the new believers in Ephesus.

> Many also of those who had believed kept coming, confessing and disclosing their practices. And many of those who practiced magic brought their books together and began burning them in the sight of all; and they counted up the price of them and found it fifty thousand pieces of silver.[7] (vv. 18–19)

What a dazzling bonfire that must have been! However, an even greater fire was blazing in the believers' hearts as they released their worldly attachments and committed themselves to the Lord.

As with the Ephesians, the Holy Spirit searches out and exposes our hidden stores of worldly souvenirs. When He does, we also must confess their existence, disclose our preoccupation with them, and then destroy them. Admittedly, the bonfire is painful and costly, but it is also freeing and gloriously life-changing.

---

7. The "pieces of silver" were drachmas. One drachma represented about a day's wage, so multiply the average daily wage in your area times fifty thousand, and you'll have our dollar equivalent. That was an expensive fire!

Application: Some Final Suggestions

With His extraordinary power, God can make some changes in your life too. Here are a couple of suggestions that will allow Him room to work.

First, remember that *hardening happens slowly and silently.* Sinful patterns often have their roots in our younger years. Although the Holy Spirit keeps reminding us of them, we sometimes ignore Him. And with each refusal, our hearts become harder and harder, so that eventually the Spirit's convictions glance off our hearts like twigs sliding across a frozen lake. Instead of turning a deaf ear, respond quickly to His prodding—deal with your sins promptly so that your heart stays soft and sensitive.

Second, *becoming pliable calls for a willingness to change.* A soft heart stays soft when we massage it with the oil of a willing attitude. God asks us merely to be open to His power, like the young woman who came to church with her suicide note already prepared. She just made one tiny step toward God, and He embraced her with His power, giving her hope.

He can do the same for you. Are you willing to let Him?

Living Insights

"To live life honestly . . ."[8] According to Larry Crabb, that's the path to knowing God and, as a result, the path to deep, inner change. However,

> far too many Christians do not deal honestly with their lives. Clichés about the power of the Word are repeated with smug piety among people who see little evidence of its life-changing impact. Affirmations concerning the role of God's Spirit in changing lives substitute for compelling personal testimony about what He is doing. Admonitions to maintain a regular devotional and prayer life are used to avoid confusing contact with the messy details of people's lives. . . . The pathway to change is more often discussed and debated than displayed.[9]

8. Larry Crabb, *Inside Out* (Colorado Springs, Colo.: NavPress, 1988), p. 220.
9. Crabb, *Inside Out*, p. 219.

Crabb says that honest living, rather than focusing on externals, probes beneath the surface to our deepest need—our inner thirst.

> The purpose of an inside look is to promote that kind of spiritual depth. The more deeply we sense our thirst, the more passionately we'll pursue water. And the more clearly we recognize how we dig our own wells in search of water, the more fully we can repent of our self-sufficiency and turn to God in obedient trust.[10]

Does your Christianity tend more toward the cliché than the real? Have you any wells of self-sufficiency you rely on to slake your thirst? Have you been protecting or denying any hidden weaknesses rather than letting God expose and transform them? Use this time for some honest reflection—God's light might be glaring at first, but He is very willing to wrap us in His forgiveness and love. And into our empty hands He places the gift of real change.

_____

_____

_____

_____

_____

_____

_____

_____

_____

_____

_____

_____

10. Crabb, *Inside Out*, p. 202.

Living Insights

In the letter we quoted at the beginning of this chapter, the young woman wrote, "The circumstances aren't vastly, horribly, wonderfully changed . . . but I am." Often we wish God would change our circumstances rather than us. It's easier to blame our problems on the situation, thinking that if only God would change them we would be happy.

What circumstances in your life do you wish God would change in order to bring you inner peace and happiness?

_____

_____

_____

God could change your circumstances with a snap of His fingers. Do you need a new job? Snap. New house? Snap. New relationships? Snap, snap, snap! But maybe He wants to change you first. What changes do you think He'd like to make in your life?

_____

_____

_____

If you're open to change, His strong but gentle hand will begin to soften and mold you so that you can face your circumstances in full honesty. His changes rarely happen overnight, but the process can begin today.

Chapter 5

PEACE IN SPITE OF PANIC

Acts 19:21–41

S halom!" Two Jewish friends greet one another with an embrace and a warm smile. More than just saying "hello," they are offering each other a blessing: "Peace be with you."

What is the nature of this *shalom*-type peace? The Bible reveals a treasure chest of its attributes: quietness, confidence, security, and rest (see Isa. 32:17–18). It depicts *shalom* as the steadiness of Daniel waiting in the lions' den, the serenity of Jesus asleep in the storm-tossed boat, the joyful singing of Paul and Silas chained together in the Philippian jail.

How do we unlock this kind of peace in our lives? The prophet Isaiah gives us the key:

> "The steadfast of mind Thou wilt keep in perfect
>   peace,
> Because he trusts in Thee.
> Trust in the Lord forever,
> For in God the Lord, we have an everlasting Rock."
> (26:3–4)

This sounds beautiful, but does it really work? Can this ancient key fit our contemporary lives? Let's take a moment to examine Isaiah's liberating words more closely.

The phrase "the steadfast of mind" is two words in Hebrew, one of which means "lean upon . . . support"[1] and the other, "state of mind."[2] The word *keep* means "watch over, protect,"[3] and that with which God does the keeping is peace, repeated in the verse for emphasis—literally *shalom, shalom* or "unending security." Put these definitions together and the line reads, "The frame of mind that is leaning on and receiving support from You, O Lord, You will protect with infinite calm." The next line tells us the impetus for this peace: our trust in God. The Hebrew word for *trust* has an Arabic cousin

---

1. R. Laird Harris, ed. *Theological Wordbook of the Old Testament* (Chicago, Ill.: Moody Press, 1980), vol. 2, p. 628.

2. Harris, ed. *Theological Wordbook of the Old Testament*, vol. 1, p. 396.

3. Harris, ed. *Theological Wordbook of the Old Testament*, vol. 2, p. 594.

that provides us a picture as well as a meaning: "to throw one down upon his face."[4]

So those who throw themselves on God, who remove all other crutches, who abandon their anxieties and fears will experience God's *shalom*. How long should we keep trusting? Until the clouds disappear? Until we can handle things ourselves? No . . . forever. And as long as we trust Him, He will be there like a timeless, immovable rock.

What a marvelous promise! And here it is, reaching up from the page of Scripture, inviting each of us to cling to it as children cling to their father's neck. One person whom we find constantly in its embrace is the apostle Paul—particularly in his final days at Ephesus.

Completing a Successful Task

Always one to complete what he started, Paul is in the process of wrapping up a fulfilling and successful ministry in Ephesus. Luke refers to those days and then points to the Apostle's plans for the future:

> Now after these things were finished, Paul purposed in the spirit to go to Jerusalem after he had passed through Macedonia and Achaia, saying, "After I have been there, I must also see Rome." (Acts 19:21)

Burning within Paul's soul is the dream of someday reaching Rome. Why is this city so important to him?

> Rome was the Oval Office of the world, the place of ultimate clout. The emperor lived there. Saints lived in Caesar's palace. Paul knew that if he could reach Rome, he could reach some of the most influential Christians of the known world. Also, quite probably, he could gain an audience with the emperor himself.[5]

What a thrilling possibility! Imagine *Caesar* bowing his knee to Jesus . . . the whole world would know the glory of Christ! Paul

---

4. William Gesenius, *A Hebrew and English Lexicon of the Old Testament*, trans. Edward Robinson (Oxford, England: Clarendon Press, n.d.), p. 105.

5. Charles R. Swindoll, *Stress Fractures* (Portland, Oreg.: Multnomah Press, 1990), p. 40.

yearns for that day, yet verse 22 shows that he is content to wait for God's timing.

> Having sent into Macedonia two of those who ministered to him, Timothy and Erastus, he himself stayed in Asia for a while.

How long did he stay in Asia? Well, we know he ministered in Ephesus a total of three years (20:31). Three months of that time, he taught in the synagogue (19:8); and for another two years, he spoke in the school of Tyrannus (v. 10). That leaves nine months that he stayed in Asia while Rome was tugging at his heart.

Paul's natural response to his unfulfilled dreams would have been frustration, anxiety, and panic, but God's peace was watching over him. As a result, he was able to wait patiently and keep working at his present tasks.

From his example, we can formulate the first of three definitions of peace: *the ability to remain faithful in spite of the panic of unfulfilled dreams.* When we lean on the Lord as an everlasting Rock, entrusting the future to Him, He supports us with His peace. Then we can stay at our posts, letting Him unlock the doors of our dreams at just the right time.

Facing an Uncontrollable Situation

Because Paul was content to wait on the Lord, surely his circumstances would remain as calm and peaceful as his attitude.

Not so.

"About that time . . ." the next verse opens, reminding us that often, just when things are settled in our hearts, just when we've stopped panicking and started trusting, a dam breaks and trouble comes flooding in.

> About that time there arose no small disturbance concerning the Way. (v. 23)

Public Accusation

The disturbance begins with an accusation.

> A certain man named Demetrius, a silversmith, who made silver shrines of Artemis, was bringing no little business to the craftsmen; these he gathered together with the workmen of similar trades, and said, "Men,

37

you know that our prosperity depends upon this business. And you see and hear that not only in Ephesus, but in almost all of Asia, this Paul has persuaded and turned away a considerable number of people, saying that gods made with hands are no gods at all." (vv. 24–26)

Demetrius, the CEO of the silversmith's guild—and a man who has never met Paul—accuses him of undermining their profitable business. Everett Harrison explains what these craftsmen were making:

The shrines were probably not statuettes of the goddess but small representations of her seated in her temple. Devotees purchased these and presented them at the temple as an act of worship.[6]

As a result of Paul's preaching and the spread of the gospel, thousands of people had begun worshiping the authentic God and had forsaken the odd-looking Artemis and her myriad of replicas and trinkets. So the market—and Demetrius' income—had plummeted.

Personal Misunderstanding

The silversmiths cared little about God's truth; they cared only about the nose-diving line on their profit charts. But was it Paul's fault that sales had slipped? Should he be blamed? He hadn't made anyone do anything; rather, God was the One changing lives. But they couldn't take a swipe at Him, so they made Paul their punching bag.

As Demetrius continues his inflammatory speech to his fellow craftsmen, the group grows angrier with each exaggerated accusation.

"And not only is there danger that this trade of ours fall into disrepute, but also that the temple of the great goddess Artemis be regarded as worthless and that she whom all of Asia and the world worship should even be dethroned from her magnificence." And when they heard this and were filled with rage, they began crying out, saying, "Great is Artemis of the Ephesians!" (vv. 27–28)

6. Everett F. Harrison, *Interpreting Acts: The Expanding Church* (Grand Rapids, Mich.: Zondervan Publishing House, Academie Books, 1986), p. 317.

Physical Threat

Goaded by fear, greed, and religious zeal, the tradesmen begin screaming and chanting. The sound of the tumult spills out into the streets.

> The city was filled with the confusion, and they rushed with one accord into the theater, dragging along Gaius and Aristarchus, Paul's traveling companions from Macedonia. (v. 29)

The situation turns suddenly dangerous as thousands of people mob together, grab Paul's companions—probably because they couldn't find him—and push their way into the theater.[7]

News of the bedlam soon reaches the Apostle, who immediately wants to enter the fray (v. 30a). "Let me at 'em!" Paul exclaims. But those around him wisely warn him not to go (vv. 30b–31).[8] Why isn't he afraid? Only God's perfect peace—His *shalom, shalom*—could have chased the fear from Paul's heart.

> When you live free of anxiety, there is an "envelope of invincibility" in your spirit. It surrounds you, and you don't sense the intimidation of a mob or the fear of peril. It's nothing short of magnificent.[9]

In the end, Paul did not venture into the theater; but his frame of mind exemplified the second definition of peace: *the ability to stay calm in spite of the panic of uncontrollable and unpleasant circumstances.*

Being at peace is no problem when our circumstances are serene. But being calm when a riot is raging at our door—that requires true peace, the kind that comes only from relying wholly upon God. He is bigger than any person or mob, and no circumstance—no matter how riotous—is out of His control.

---

7. This theater still exists and is more like a stadium or open-air amphitheater. It can hold at least twenty-five thousand people, all of them, by this time, part of a powder keg of hostility about to explode. See John Stott, *The Spirit, the Church, and the World: The Message of Acts* (Downers Grove, Ill.: InterVarsity Press, 1990), p. 309.

8. In verse 31, Luke refers to "Asiarchs." These friends of Paul "were leading citizens, who were prominent members of the provincial council of Asia." Stott, *Spirit, Church, and World,* p. 310.

9. Swindoll, *Stress Fractures,* p. 45.

Waiting through Uncertain Moments

While Paul continues to wait on the Lord, the situation seems to deteriorate even more.

> So then, some were shouting one thing and some another, for the assembly was in confusion, and the majority did not know for what cause they had come together. (v. 32)

There is so much confusion and mayhem that the people don't even know what they're supposed to be angry about! Then, to make matters worse, some Jews convince one of their leaders, Alexander, to try to calm the crowd and make it clear that they aren't the ones to blame. But seeing a monotheistic Jew only incites the people's polytheistic zeal. "Great is Artemis of the Ephesians," they shout over and over again for two full hours (vv. 33b–34).

All the while, Paul remains hidden, his life in more and more danger with each passing minute. The pressure is rising, but at the right moment, the God whom Paul serves and trusts sends in—the cavalry? A high Roman official?

No, just the town clerk.[10]

> After quieting the multitude, the town clerk said, "Men of Ephesus, what man is there after all who does not know that the city of the Ephesians is guardian of the temple of the great Artemis, and of the image which fell down from heaven? Since then these are undeniable facts, you ought to keep calm and to do nothing rash. For you have brought these men here who are neither robbers of temples nor blasphemers of our goddess. So then, if Demetrius and the craftsmen who are with him have a complaint against any man, the courts are in session and proconsuls are available; let them bring charges against one another. But if you want anything beyond this, it shall be settled in the lawful assembly.

---

10. According to F. F. Bruce, he was the "secretary of the city, the executive officer who published the decrees of the civic assembly. . . . He acted as liaison officer between the civic administration and the Roman provincial administration." *Commentary on the Book of the Acts,* The New International Commentary on the New Testament, F. F. Bruce, ed. (Grand Rapids, Mich.: William B. Eerdmans Publishing Co., 1954), pp. 400–401.

For indeed we are in danger of being accused of a riot in connection with today's affair, since there is no real cause for it; and in this connection we shall be unable to account for this disorderly gathering." And after saying this he dismissed the assembly. (vv. 35–41)

Knowing that his job was on the line, this clerk carefully selected a few facts and reminders about proper legal channels and preserved his own job, the city's standing, and most of all, the disciples' lives.

As if He were playing chess, God moved a pawn into just the right square to block Paul's opponent. In our lives also, He has a way of arranging unexpected events and unlikely people to defend us. We just have to wait for Him to make His move.

This episode then provides us the third definition of peace: *the ability to wait patiently in spite of panic brought on by uncertainty.* In times of fear, remember God's peaceful promise:

Trust in the Lord with all your heart,
And do not lean on your own understanding.
In all your ways acknowledge Him,
And He will make your paths straight.
(Prov. 3:5–6)

A Concluding Thought

Why do we have so little peace? Because we want to be in charge of our lives. We want to accomplish our own dreams, control uncontrollable situations, and manipulate our uncertain futures. This way of thinking, though, leads us down the miry path of worry and panic.

In contrast, as Isaiah reminds us, people who rely on God experience perpetual peace. Trust . . . it's the only way to find peace amidst the anxiety of the world. May this kind of peace be with you. *Shalom!*

 *Living Insights*

On any given day, our frame of mind, like the weather, can be warm and sunny with only a slight chance of rain, or it can be overcast and cold with storm clouds billowing on the horizon.

What accounts for this variability? A good deal has to do with whether we are trusting in the Lord. People at peace trust the Lord, and conversely, people who trust the Lord are at peace (see Isa. 26:3).

What's your weather like today? Take a moment to check your heart's barometer, and write down your own weather report.

_____

_____

_____

You may not be able to change the weather, but you can change your frame of mind. No matter how tempestuous it is outside, no matter how your circumstances swirl and crash around you, you can kindle a warm fire of inner peace. The key is in trusting the Lord— the subject of the next Living Insight.

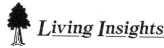 *Living Insights*

Can you trust God? This question is the title of the first chapter in Jerry Bridges' book *Trusting God,* and it is a good place to begin exploring the subject. But before you attempt to answer it, understand that the question has two possible meanings.

> Can you *trust* God, i.e., is He dependable in times of adversity? But the second meaning is also critical, can *you* trust God? Do you have such a relationship with God and such a confidence in Him that you believe He is with you in your adversity even though you do not see any evidence of His presence and His power?[11]

The first meaning is objective: Is God trustworthy? The second is subjective: Can I and, equally important, will I trust Him?

Let's examine the first side of the question. From the following verses, in what ways is God trustworthy?

Psalm 33:4 *What God says is true, and what He does is always faithful.*

Psalm 91:1–2 _____

11. Jerry Bridges, *Trusting God* (Colorado Springs, Colo.: NavPress, 1988), p. 16.

Psalm 100:5 _____

Lamentations 3:22–23 _____

2 Timothy 2:13 _____

From Scripture, we know that God is loving and faithful—it is impossible for Him to betray us. Yet what we feel about God may be different. We may feel that He has abandoned us or forgotten us, and those feelings determine the answer to the second side of the question: Can *you* trust God?

Have there been some experiences in your past that have caused you to doubt God's trustworthiness? If so, what happened?

_____

_____

_____

How did those experiences inhibit your ability to trust God?

_____

_____

_____

How wonderful it would be if God would give each of us a vision of Himself—then trusting Him would be easy. In heaven, we will see Him face to face, but until then, we will wrestle with our doubts and our feelings. If trusting God is difficult for you, admit that to Him. Express to Him your feelings, then through His Word listen to His comfort and encouragement (see Pss. 56:8; 147:3; Isa. 41:13; 1 Pet. 5:7). You can learn to trust God.[12]

---

12. In addition to Bridges' book, two other resources on this subject are *Disappointment with God*, by Philip Yancey (Grand Rapids, Mich.: Zondervan Publishing House, 1988); and *When You Can't Come Back*, by Dave and Jan Dravecky with Ken Gire (Grand Rapids, Mich.: Zondervan Publishing House; San Francisco, Calif.: HarperSanFrancisco, 1992).

Chapter 6

SAILING, SPEAKING, AND SLEEPING IN CHURCH

Acts 20:1–12

In 1 Corinthians 15:32, the apostle Paul makes a cryptic yet incisive reference to his time in Ephesus:

I fought with wild beasts at Ephesus.[1]

What an apt description of the frenzied riot he and his companions had just endured! Snarling and angry, Demetrius and his mob were ready to tear them all apart in a bloody rage. Fortunately, though, God used a simple town clerk to quiet them down and restore reason. So what had crescendoed to a roar soon dissipated into a shuffling murmur as the people went home.

With peace reestablished and the growing church safe, Paul now decides that the time is right to move on. As he packs his bags and charts a course to Macedonia, let's join him and see what other adventures await him around the next bend in the road.

Leaving Ephesus, Ministering in Macedonia

Paul has laced up his sandals and his knapsack is by the door, but before he sets off, he has one last task to tie up.

> And after the uproar had ceased, Paul sent for the disciples and *when he had exhorted them* and taken his leave of them, he departed to go to Macedonia. (Acts 20:1, emphasis added)

After three years of ministry in Ephesus, a sizable number of disciples have been raised up. Evangelism isn't what's crucial now, but exhortation. Let's take a closer look at what may be an unfamiliar term.

---

1. As a Roman citizen, Paul could not have been literally thrown to the beasts in the coliseum. So we are safe in assuming that this is a figurative reference.

Exhortation

Since we don't often use the word *exhortation*,[2] we may not be exactly sure of what it means. Here's a simple definition: "the ability to apply revealed truth to life." Counselors, for instance, who can skillfully extract principles from Scripture and show people how to employ them in their lives, have this spiritual gift.

An exhortation can be a warning, a comforting statement, or an encouraging comment. And its value is inestimable. Two proverbs highlight the treasure in this gift:

A man has joy in an apt answer,
And how delightful is a timely word!
(Prov. 15:23)

Like apples of gold in settings of silver
Is a word spoken in right circumstances.
(25:11)

Exhortation was a gift Paul had, and he paused to employ it before leaving the Ephesians and going to Macedonia.

Departure

With his counsel given and his good-byes said, he sets off for Macedonia, following the coastal route north to Troas and then across to the Macedonian shore by ship. Once there, he visits the cities from his second missionary journey, retracing his steps through Philippi, Thessalonica, and Berea, nurturing and exhorting the infant churches he had parented years earlier.[3] Then, with his dream of reaching Rome still burning in his heart, Paul heads for the next stop on his journey: Greece (Acts 20:2).

At Greece, on to Troas

Paul has a fruitful three-month stay in Greece, during which he writes his doctrinal masterpiece, the Epistle to the Romans. From

---

2. The Greek word for *exhort* is *parakaleō*—a word which literally means, "to call alongside, to help." In this same sense, the Holy Spirit is a *paraklētos*, a helper or comforter (John 14:26).

3. Paul spent about a year in Macedonia and possibly used this time to preach the gospel as far west as Illyricum, an area in what until recently was called Yugoslavia (Rom. 15:19). Also during his stay there, he wrote two of his epistles—2 Corinthians and possibly Galatians, though many scholars date the writing of Galatians after the first missionary journey and the place of origin as Antioch of Syria. He had already written two letters to the Corinthian believers from Ephesus—one letter that has been lost and another that is our 1 Corinthians.

that letter, we read that he has been collecting donations from the churches in Macedonia and Achaia for the needy believers in Jerusalem (see Rom. 15:25–26), where he is hoping to go before Passover. However, his plans for an ocean crossing hit some murderous swells.

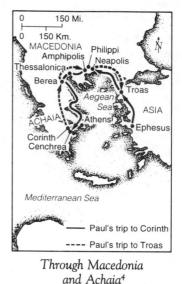

> A plot was formed against him by the Jews as he was about to set sail for Syria, [so] he determined to return through Macedonia. (Acts 20:3b)

Apparently, the vengeful Jews wanted to "assassinate him on board ship and dispose of his body at sea."[5] But when Paul sensed this ill wind blowing,

Through Macedonia and Achaia[4]

he wisely set a different course, back up through Macedonia, the way he had just come.

Does this evasive maneuver mean that Paul didn't trust God to protect him on the ship? Did he show a lack of courage by changing his travel route? Not at all! Paul would have been foolish to board that ship; God had informed him of the plot so he could escape the assassination attempt, not so his courage could be tested. Paul trusted God, but he also knew when to retreat from danger.

Accompanying him back through Macedonia were

> Sopater of Berea, the son of Pyrrhus; and . . . Aristarchus and Secundus of the Thessalonians; and Gaius of Derbe, and Timothy; and Tychicus and Trophimus of Asia. (v. 4)

This group of men made a sort of traveling seminary. Class was always in session as they walked along discussing the Scriptures with the Apostle. And Paul's life was always on display, exemplifying

4. Maps ©1986, 1988 are taken from the *Life Application Bible* © 1988, 1989, 1990, 1991 by Tyndale House Publishers, Inc., Wheaton, IL 60189. Used by permission. All rights reserved. *Life Application* is a trademark of Tyndale House Publishers, Inc.

5. Stanley D. Toussaint, "Acts," in *The Bible Knowledge Commentary*, New Testament edition (Wheaton, Ill.: SP Publications, Victor Books, 1983), p. 412.

how to be accessible to others—this made his teaching real.

Also, in his choice of traveling companions Paul revealed that there is no rank or hierarchy in the family of God. Ray Stedman brings this to light for us.

> The man whose name was Secundus, which means "the second," was obviously a slave. Slaves did not bother to name their children; they just numbered them—the first, the second, the third, and so on. It may be that "number three," Tertius, who wrote the Letter to the Romans as Paul's secretary [see Rom. 16:22], was this man's brother.[6]

Secundus' slave status made as little difference to Paul as Sopater's noble heritage and famous father. Even Timothy was half Jewish and half Gentile—yet Paul freely accepted him too. Some of the men were from Asia, some from Europe . . . Paul treated them all as brothers in Christ. He lived out the truths he wrote to others:

> There is neither Jew nor Greek, there is neither slave nor free man, there is neither male nor female; for you are all one in Christ Jesus. (Gal. 3:28)

With this group of men, Paul continued to move from city to city, eventually linking up with Luke in Philippi. This is indicated by Luke's use of the pronouns *us* and *we* in the account.[7]

> These had gone on ahead and were waiting for us at Troas. And we sailed from Philippi after the days of Unleavened Bread, and came to them at Troas within five days; and there we stayed seven days. (Acts 20:5–6)

Apparently, Luke and Paul stayed in Philippi to celebrate Passover with the believers there, then met up with the other men, who had already crossed over to Troas.

---

6. Ray Stedman, *Acts 13–20: Growth of the Body* (Santa Ana, Calif.: Vision House Publishers, 1976), p. 188.

7. The other "we" sections in Acts are: 16:10–17; 21:1–18; and 27:1–28:16.

Events at Troas

This brief, seven-day visit in Troas must have been nostalgic for Paul. For it was here that God had given him the vision of the Macedonian man calling out to him, "Come over to Macedonia and help us" (16:9). And now he had the opportunity to minister in the city that had so significantly impacted his life.

Portrait of Worship in the Early Church

In describing the events at Troas, Luke provides us a rare glimpse of first-century church life.

> On the first day of the week, when we were gathered together to break bread, Paul began talking to them, intending to depart the next day, and he prolonged his message until midnight. (20:7)

Four facets of their worship are especially outstanding in this verse. First, we notice on what day of the week the early church met to worship. The Jews observed the Sabbath on the seventh day, Saturday. But the Christians met on the first day of the week, Sunday—in honor, we assume, of the day of Jesus' resurrection (Matt. 28:1ff).

Second, "we were gathered together" implies that the church service was primarily a time for believers. On Sundays, Christians would meet to spiritually tool up for the week ahead, when they would be in the world witnessing for Christ.

Third, the Lord's Supper was an integral part of their worship. Luke simply writes, "we were gathered together to break bread." This phrase gives us no details concerning how they celebrated communion, which is a good thing, because now we are free to remember Christ's death in a variety of ways. We do not have to be in a church building, and the clergy doesn't necessarily have to administer it. As long as there is a worshipful spirit, a body of believers can partake of the Lord's Supper anywhere and in any manner.

The final glimpse of church life Luke shows us is the presence of biblical teaching. "Paul began talking to them," and he talked and talked and talked! In fact, he kept teaching until midnight—showing us that an adequate feeding of the saints requires a significant period of time to properly unfold the truth. Admittedly, Paul got a little carried away here, which had an unfortunate effect on a tired boy named Eutychus.

Snapshot of a Sleepy Saint

> There were many lamps in the upper room where
> we were gathered together. And there was a certain
> young man named Eutychus sitting on the window
> sill, sinking into a deep sleep; and as Paul kept on
> talking, he was overcome by sleep and fell down from
> the third floor, and was picked up dead. But Paul
> went down and fell upon him and after embracing
> him, he said, "Do not be troubled, for his life is in
> him." And when he had gone back up, and had
> broken the bread and eaten, he talked with them a
> long while, until daybreak, and so departed. And
> they took away the boy alive, and were greatly com-
> forted. (Acts 20:8–12)

Poor Eutychus . . . not only does he nod off while listening to
the great apostle Paul, but he tips over and falls right out of a third-
story window! Most embarrassing, though, is that Luke records this
event so every generation across the entire world can read about it.

Why do people fall asleep in church? Basically, there are five
reasons:

(1) *Tradition:* When we were youngsters, our parents unwittingly
    taught us to associate sermons with sleep when they allowed
    us to nap in their laps.

(2) *Physical factors:* Sometimes the church can be stuffy, poorly
    ventilated, and dimly lit—too warm and dark to keep us
    from feeling drowsy. This probably played a part in Eutychus'
    case, with the flickering lamps casting hypnotizing shadows
    and raising the temperature of the room.

(3) *Personal factors:* Occasionally, we don't get enough sleep the
    night before, or perhaps we're taking some medication or
    have a health problem that causes sleepiness.

(4) *Indifference:* This is just a plain lack of interest in spiritual
    things, with causes ranging from preoccupation to resent-
    ment.

(5) *Boring preacher:* Poorly organized, rambling material; a
    monotone delivery; too much time spent on needless detail;

being out of touch with people's needs—which of us hasn't struggled to stay awake while listening to preaching like this!

As people called to communicate Jesus Christ wherever we are, we need to be especially sensitive about this last cause. We would do well to heed the words of Solomon:

> In addition to being a wise man, the Preacher also taught the people knowledge; and he pondered, searched out and arranged many proverbs. The Preacher sought to find delightful words and to write words of truth correctly.
> The words of wise men are like goads, and masters of these collections are like well-driven nails; they are given by one Shepherd. (Eccles. 12:9–11)

When we teach, we should take great care to find the right words that will act as goads in the lives of the people who listen to us, stimulating and urging them into action—not sleep.

Thankfully, in Eutychus' case, his sleep is not permanent. In yet another revelation of God's miraculous grace, Paul embraces the young man and life returns to his body. Spiritually speaking, the gospel has that same power to invigorate souls that are dead in sin. Through faith, we can come to life and spread the word about Christ's sustaining power.

Application for Today

On this leg of his third missionary journey, Paul has led us from Ephesus, through Macedonia and Greece, and back to Troas in Asia. Although he has much left to teach us about Christian maturity in his upcoming travels, for now, three main lessons shine through his life.

First, *to strengthen others' lives, encouragement is essential.* The writer to the Hebrews capsulized Paul's example:

> Let us consider how to stimulate one another to love and good deeds, not forsaking our own assembling together, as is the habit of some, but encouraging one another; and all the more, as you see the day drawing near. (10:24–25)

Second, *encouraging one another calls for availability.* Paul taught his group of men by being close to them. As a result, God's truth

50

rubbed off on their lives, changing the way they thought and acted.

Third, *being available includes communication*. Paul communicated Scripture in his actions as well as his words. He was a writer and a speaker—two crafts available to us today. If God has given you skills for writing or speaking, hone them well. Study the Scripture closely. Listen to God's voice intently. And learn how to prepare your words so that they will be like a banquet to your audience, appealing and delicious, sure to satisfy.

Living Insights

Exhorting others is like lighting small fires in people's lives. Sometimes the fires illumine sin, drawing people toward repentance. Sometimes they awaken sleepers, stirring them to action. Sometimes they warm weary travelers, comforting them with biblical truth. And sometimes they spark failing hearts, encouraging them with hope.

Do you think you are an exhorter? Perhaps the Holy Spirit has given this spiritual gift to you in latent form and you need to develop it. If so, you can have no better teacher than Paul.

In 1 Corinthians 11:17–22, Paul lights a fire under some complacent and sinful believers. Write down what you observe about his exhortation technique. We'll start you off with one example.

He prepares them for his admonishment by saying, "I do not praise you."

_____

_____

_____

_____

In Galatians 1:6–9, he awakens some sleepers. Write down how he lights this fire.

_____

_____

In 2 Thessalonians 1:3–4, he comforts his readers. Again, write down his technique.

_____

_____

In 1 Corinthians 15:50–58, he encourages the people with hope. How does he do this?

_____

_____

Is there someone you know who needs one of these fires of exhortation lit in his or her life? Using Paul's technique as a model, formulate what to say to this person in the space provided. As you do, examine your own motives, making sure that what you say is out of love. And when you finish your thoughts, pray that the Holy Spirit will give you the opportunity to light the fire in the right place, at the right time.

_____

_____

_____

_____

_____

_____

_____

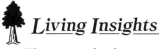 Living Insights

The type of exhortation that is most needed and perhaps most absent in our churches is encouragement. Psychologist Larry Crabb recalls a time as a teenager when some encouraging words sparked hope in his life.

> It was customary in our congregation to encourage young men to enter into the privilege of worship by standing and praying aloud. That particular Sunday I sensed the pressure of the saints (not, I fear, the leading of the Spirit), and I responded by unsteadily

leaving my chair, for the first time, with the intention of praying.

Filled less with worship than with nervousness, I found my theology becoming confused to the point of heresy. I remember thanking the Father for hanging on the cross and praising Christ for triumphantly bringing the Spirit from the grave. Stuttering throughout, I finally thought of the word *Amen* (perhaps the first evidence of the Spirit's leading), said it, and sat down. I recall staring at the floor, too embarrassed to look around, and solemnly vowing *never again* to pray or speak aloud in front of a group.

. . .

When the service was over, I darted toward the door, not wishing to encounter an elder who might feel obliged to correct my twisted theology. But I was not quick enough. An older Christian man named Jim Dunbar intercepted me, put his arm on my shoulder, and cleared his throat. . . .

"Larry," he said, "there's one thing I want you to know. Whatever you do for the Lord, I'm behind you one thousand percent." Then he walked away.

Even as I write these words, my eyes fill with tears. I have yet to tell that story to an audience without at least mildly choking. Those words were life words. They had power. They reached deep into my being. . . .

. . . Not only death, but also life lies in the power of the tongue.[8]

You, too, have life-words to give someone—your spouse, your friend, your child. Won't you give them today?

8. Larry Crabb, *Encouragement: The Key to Caring* (Grand Rapids, Mich.: Zondervan Publishing House, Pyranee Books, 1984), pp. 24–25.

Chapter 7

A TOUCHING FAREWELL

Acts 20:13–38

Marc 12, 1942 . . .

In an emotionally charged moment, President Franklin D. Roosevelt ordered General Douglas MacArthur to leave the Philippines, where he had been commanding a futile defensive against the overwhelming and relentless Japanese military. Obeying that order meant leaving his friend General Jonathan Wainwright and thirty-six thousand men stranded on the Bataan Peninsula. Short on supplies, they were already on half rations. A crushing defeat at the hands of the brutal enemy was inevitable.

As a military officer trained to stick by his men, the thought of abandoning his post tore him up inside. But he had his orders—he had to go. While boarding the boat to leave, he turned to view the once lush shoreline cratered by months of shelling, and he thought of the men and their fate in the Japanese torture camps. Full of both grit and choked emotion, his farewell was simply, "I shall return."

In this passage of Acts, that same emotion laces Paul's words as he says good-bye to some dear friends, the elders of the church at Ephesus. He knows he is leaving them vulnerable to the enemy attacks of false teaching and spiritual oppression. But unlike MacArthur, he cannot promise to return and defend them, for he knows he will never see them again. This, then, is his final farewell.

A Geographical Survey: From Troas to Miletus

Having just completed a one-week stay in Troas, Paul now journeys on toward Miletus—a small port town where he will say good-bye to his friends in Ephesus. Traveling with him are a group of representatives from several churches in Europe and Asia, whose mission it is to help deliver the money their congregations have donated to the needy believers in Jerusalem (see Acts 20:4 and Rom. 15:25–26). Luke, a member of the traveling party, describes the four-day voyage from Troas to Miletus.

We, going ahead to the ship, set sail for Assos,

intending from there to take Paul on board; for thus he had arranged it, intending himself to go by land. And when he met us at Assos, we took him on board and came to Mitylene. And sailing from there, we arrived the following day opposite Chios; and the next day we crossed over to Samos; and the day following we came to Miletus. For Paul had decided to sail past Ephesus in order that he might not have to spend time in Asia; for he was hurrying to be in Jerusalem, if possible, on the day of Pentecost.

Paul Travels from Troas to Miletus[1]

And from Miletus he sent to Ephesus and called to him the elders of the church. (Acts 20:13–17)

Expositional Study: From Paul to Elders

What little time Paul has in Miletus, he wants to spend with the church elders, who must travel about thirty-five miles south to meet him (v. 17).

What will Paul say to these men whom he has nurtured from spiritual infancy? Surely, as he looks out on the small group, he recalls the joyful day when each one of them embraced Jesus as his Lord. Memories flood his thoughts as he formulates what will become his last and most vital words to them—words as from a father to the sons he knows he will never see again.

Characteristics of a Healthy Ministry

Paul begins slowly, taking the elders back to the days when he lived and worked among them.

---

1. Maps © 1986, 1988 are taken from the *Life Application Bible* © 1988, 1989, 1990, 1991 by Tyndale House Publishers, Inc., Wheaton, IL 60189. Used by permission. All rights reserved. *Life Application* is a trademark of Tyndale House Publishers, Inc.

"You yourselves know, from the first day that I set foot in Asia, how I was with you the whole time, serving the Lord with all humility and with tears and with trials which came upon me through the plots of the Jews; how I did not shrink from declaring to you anything that was profitable, and teaching you publicly and from house to house." (vv. 18b–20)

From this conversation, we can pick up some characteristics of Paul's work that will help us emulate his healthy ministry.

First: *Paul endured the tests of the flesh*. We can identify at least five of these tests in his words to the elders.

1. He endured the test of laziness, for he said, "from the first day . . . I was with you the whole time." From the moment he arrived in the city, he diligently worked among the people.

2. Another test he endured was pride, for he was "serving the Lord with all humility" and thereby safeguarding the effectiveness of the church as a whole.

3. He also endured the test of discouragement, for he ministered "with tears and with trials," never giving in and giving up.

4. He endured the test of fear. "I did not shrink from declaring to you anything that was profitable," Paul says, showing us that he was not intimidated by others.

5. Finally, he endured the test of fads. He employed only helpful techniques in his ministry—techniques that would edify and equip, not just impress or draw crowds.

Second: *Paul's ministry was based on solid Christian doctrine*. Referring to his teaching ministry, he says that he declared what was profitable,

"solemnly testifying to both Jews and Greeks of repentance toward God and faith in our Lord Jesus Christ." (v. 21)

Whether he was speaking to Jews or Greeks, he did not water down the truth but consistently served the people the nourishing meat of God's Word. In recalling this feature of his ministry, he was telling the elders, "Don't feed the church prepackaged philosophy. Stick to the basics of 'repentance toward God and faith in our Lord Jesus Christ.'"

Third: *Paul's ministry was free of deception and personal politics.* Concluding his recollections of his days in Ephesus, he says,

> "Therefore I testify to you this day, that I am innocent of the blood of all men. For I did not shrink from declaring to you the whole purpose of God." (vv. 26–27)

Refraining from double-talk and false information, he was "innocent of the blood of all men." In other words, according to R. C. H. Lenski,

> On the great judgment day none of the lost from this territory shall be able to point to Paul and say that his is the guilt.[2]

Even personal politics didn't enter into his teaching. He declared to them "the whole purpose of God"—not just the parts that would win votes. He balanced his topics between the sweet and the sour, teaching *all* of God's revelation, regardless of the people's likes and dislikes.

Notice, also, what Paul doesn't mention. He doesn't reminisce on the signs of health that we normally look for, such as spiraling growth figures and impressive building programs. Neither does he use this opportunity to get back at those who injured him. Instead, as he reflects on the past, he emphasizes the positive qualities of the ministry so that the elders will continue his legacy into the future—a future that for Paul is clouded with uncertainty.

Admission of an Uncertain Future

In this portion of his talk, Paul ushers his friends into his heart of hearts, revealing his deepest thoughts and his solid faith.

> "And now, behold, bound in spirit, I am on my way to Jerusalem, not knowing what will happen to me there, except that the Holy Spirit solemnly testifies to me in every city, saying that bonds and afflictions await me." (vv. 22–23)

Despite the dangerous waters ahead, he doesn't waver from his

---

2. R. C. H. Lenski, *The Interpretation of the Acts of the Apostles* (Columbus, Ohio: Wartburg Press, 1944), p. 845.

decision to travel to Jerusalem. He won't wait for the forecast to improve before he launches off into God's will, for he knows that even when a believer follows God closely, difficulties may lie ahead. But how can he be so brave? Only by focusing on Christ rather than himself can he pacify the waves of uncertainty in his soul.

> "But I do not consider my life of any account as dear to myself, in order that I may finish my course, and the ministry which I received from the Lord Jesus, to testify solemnly of the gospel of the grace of God. And now, behold, I know that all of you, among whom I went about preaching the kingdom, will see my face no more." (vv. 24–25)

One purpose propelled Paul's life: "to testify solemnly of the gospel of the grace of God." Nothing else mattered—not his reputation, his comfort, or even his own safety. He had died to self so that he could live for Christ . . . even if it meant Jerusalem and chains.

Perils of a Growing Church

Realizing that difficulties lurk just around the corner for the Ephesian Christians as well, Paul warns them of the dangers ahead.

First, he warns them of *the peril of personal blind spots*. He implies this at the beginning of verse 28:

> "*Be on guard for yourselves* and for all the flock, among which the Holy Spirit has made you overseers, to shepherd the church of God which He purchased with His own blood." (emphasis added)

Odd advice for a healthy church? On the contrary, good health today cannot be taken for granted as good health tomorrow. If the elders neglect their spiritual leadership role, the flock may stray from the Lord.[3] Without warning, they may slip into a crevice of rigid legalism or a slough of comfortable apathy.

Second, there's *the peril of external attack*.

> "I know that after my departure savage wolves will come in among you, not sparing the flock." (v. 29)

---

3. Sadly, the Ephesian church did stray from the Lord. In John's Revelation, Christ indicted the people, saying, "I have this against you, that you have left your first love" (Rev. 2:4; see also v. 1a).

58

As shepherds, the elders must be on the lookout for false teachers and cult leaders who love to invade growing churches. Third, he cautions them about *the peril of internal corruption*.

"And from among your own selves men will arise, speaking perverse things, to draw away the disciples after them." (v. 30)

They must not become satisfied with their current success, because they can still become weak and disintegrate from the inside out.

And fourth, challenging them with his own high standards, he forewarns them about *the peril of financial greed*.

"Therefore be on the alert, remembering that night and day for a period of three years I did not cease to admonish each one with tears. . . . I have coveted no one's silver or gold or clothes. You yourselves know that these hands ministered to my own needs and to the men who were with me. In everything I showed you that by working hard in this manner you must help the weak and remember the words of the Lord Jesus, that He Himself said, 'It is more blessed to give than to receive.'" (vv. 31, 33–35)

Even as he speaks, Paul is traveling with several men for safety as well as accountability. And he wants these Ephesian elders to emulate that kind of financial responsibility.

Essentially, though, none of Paul's warnings would take effect apart from God's grace in their lives. So Paul commits them to the Lord:

"And now I commend you to God and to the word of His grace, which is able to build you up and to give you the inheritance among all those who are sanctified." (v. 32)

Scene of Final Farewell

With his flags of warning raised and the elders committed to God, Paul is ready to depart. But before boarding the ship,

he knelt down and prayed with them all. And they began to weep aloud and embraced Paul, and repeatedly kissed him, grieving especially over the word which he had spoken, that they should see his face no more. And they were accompanying him to the ship. (vv. 36b–38)

A few years ago, he had come to them as a stranger; now he leaves them as an eternal friend. He would never see them again, that is true, but he would write them a letter—the Epistle to the Ephesians—one that we still read today, one penned by a missionary in chains to his beloved children.

Practical Significance: From Then to Now

From Paul's example, we must keep in mind two principles: (1) reflecting on the past calls for honesty and objectivity so that we can learn from it; and (2) enjoying success includes constant awareness of perils. Because spiritual health today is no guarantee of spiritual health tomorrow, we need to consciously and consistently sustain the character traits that foster holiness. Although a farewell is often teary, it can be a milestone moment—a time when we can learn from the past and forever change our future.

 Living Insights STUDY ONE

According to *Webster's*, one of the meanings of the word *abandon* is "to give (oneself) over unrestrainedly."[4] Parachutists abandon themselves when they step out of a plane; bungee jumpers abandon themselves when they leap from a bridge . . . But these people demonstrate a special kind of abandon—reckless abandon. Do you think that Paul was reckless when he abandoned himself to God and sailed into a life-threatening future at Jerusalem? Actually, in his mind he wasn't reckless at all, for his perspective of God eliminated the risk. God, after all, is more reliable than any parachute and stronger than any bungee cord.

As you read the following verses, write down Paul's view of God.

Romans 8:35–39 _____

Ephesians 3:20–21 _____

1 Timothy 6:15–16 _____

---

4. *Webster's Ninth New Collegiate Dictionary*, see "abandon."

His attitude toward life and death was based upon his knowledge of God. From the following verses, write down what you notice about that attitude.

Acts 20:24 _____

Romans 14:7–8 _____

Galatians 2:20 _____

Philippians 1:20–21 _____

Certainly, Paul's strong commitment to God did not develop overnight. It was a process of abandoning himself to God in little things, day by day. In what small ways is God asking you to step out in faith, abandoning yourself to Him?

_____

_____

_____

_____

_____

🌲 Living Insights   STUDY TWO

Are you volunteering to help at your church or in a particular Christian organization? If so, here's a simple self-diagnostic exam that is based on Paul's model of a healthy ministry. Circle the number by the answer that best fits your attitude.

- How would you rate your level of effort in your ministry?

    1. I get by with the least possible amount of work and preparation.

    2. I do my job, but I rarely do more than I'm asked.

    3. I try to do the best I can and look for ways to improve.

- In what ways is pride affecting your attitude?

    1. To be honest, I volunteered for this ministry to better my reputation.

2. As I minister, I often wonder what others are thinking about me.

3. My basic motivation is to serve the Lord.

• When you are criticized, what is your level of discouragement?

1. I often consider quitting.

2. I participate, but my heart is not in it.

3. I feel pain, but I also feel God's acceptance of me and my work.

• How do you deal with intimidation?

1. I protect myself by finding excuses to stay away.

2. I keep on the job, but I am as inconspicuous as possible.

3. I do what needs to be done, knowing that God's opinion of me is what counts.

• How do you view the latest ministry fads?

1. I usually latch on to new methods.

2. Although I see faults in the faddish methods, I still use them and try to adapt them as best I can.

3. I examine all available methods and use only those that most effectively communicate the truths of Scripture.

Everyone at one time or another has had to circle the first answers on this test. If you circled several of them, in what ways can you begin to cultivate a healthier attitude and ministry soon?

_____

_____

_____

_____

_____

Chapter 8

MAN'S ADVICE VERSUS GOD'S VOICE

Acts 21:1–17

W hat should I do, Lord?"

We've all gasped that prayer, usually in the midst of life-changing decisions such as whether to accept an out-of-town job offer, how to school our children, or if, when, and whom to marry. As we face quandaries like these, we may have even fantasized about returning to the Old Testament days when God audibly instructed his people. Like Joshua, we'd stand straight and tall before our Captain as soldiers ready to receive His orders . . .

"Here's what I want you to do," God would say in our wishful fantasy. "March around this girl's house once every day for seven days."

"Yes, yes. Go on."

"On the seventh day, march around it seven times . . . then pop the question. Her defenses will crumble and you shall have a wife."

"Yes Sir!" we'd say with a snappy salute. And off we'd go to do His will.

But God doesn't speak to us today like he spoke to Joshua. Still, we long for some kind of audible instruction—so when we have to make a major decision, we often seek advice from human sources. Unfortunately, that can complicate matters even more: sometimes the counsel, no matter how well-intentioned, conflicts with God's will.

Conflicting Advice concerning God's Will

In our lives there are three sources of advice that can lead us astray. First, we can receive erroneous *advice from our own consciences*. Although Jiminy Cricket reminds us from childhood to let our conscience be our guide, our conscience is not always trustworthy. For example, when God commanded Moses via the burning bush to deliver the enslaved Hebrews from the Egyptians, what did Moses' conscience tell him at first? It reminded him of his failure

63

forty years earlier when he killed the Egyptian taskmaster. Guilt crippled his confidence and he replied, "Who am I, that I should go to Pharaoh?" (Exod. 3:11a). His conscience was in conflict with God's will.

Second, there is the faulty *advice from other people*. On the one hand, the proverb says,

> Where there is no guidance, the people fall,
> But in abundance of counselors there is victory.
> (Prov. 11:14)

But on the other hand, people can be deceived and their wisdom defective. After the Babylonian exile, God told Nehemiah to rebuild the Jerusalem wall. Nehemiah obeyed, but certain so-called counselors protested, "What is this thing you are doing? Are you rebelling against the king?" (Neh. 2:19b). They also questioned his motives (6:6–7) and advised him wrongly to flee for his life into the temple (vv. 10–14). Sometimes counsel may sound convincing, but it can still be wrong.

Third, we can receive fallible *advice from tradition and logic*. Tradition told Jonah, "Jews don't associate with pagans like the Ninevites." And logic said, "It's impossible for this many people to repent before God destroys them." But God had told him directly, "Arise, go to Ninevah" (Jon. 1:2a). Tragically for him, he sided with tradition and logic, and what resulted was a whale of a problem for poor Jonah.

Listening to advice can lead to trouble. However, sometimes God does communicate His will to us through our consciences, the advice of others, and common sense borne out by tradition and logic. So how do we know when to follow these sources of advice and when not to? The apostle Paul faced a problem like this when, on his way to Jerusalem, he confronted a bulwark of advice that conflicted with what he thought God wanted him to do.

Differing Opinions concerning Paul's Future

You'll recall that "he was hurrying to be in Jerusalem, if possible, on the day of Pentecost" (Acts 20:16b). Even though the Holy Spirit had warned him of the trouble that awaited him there (v. 23), he was determined to press on. So the first set of opinions he had to consider was his own.

Paul, Himself

Why was Paul convinced that he should go to Jerusalem? First, he wanted to personally deliver the money donated by the churches. Second, he said that he was "bound in spirit" to go to Jerusalem (v. 22) to preach the gospel to the Jews gathered for the Pentecost celebration. In other words, he sensed the Holy Spirit driving him onward. That's why, as we read Luke's diary of the trip, there is a sense of urgency.

> And when it came about that we had parted from them and had set sail, we ran a straight course to Cos and the next day to Rhodes and from there to Patara; and having found a ship crossing over to Phoenicia, we went aboard and set sail. And when we had come in sight of Cyprus, leaving it on the left, we kept sailing to Syria and landed at Tyre; for there the ship was to unload its cargo. (21:1–3)

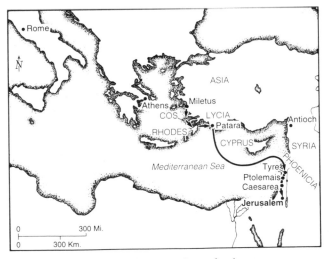

Paul Returns to Jerusalem[1]

The closer he came to Jerusalem, the more determined he was to witness for Christ there. But in Tyre, he began hearing objections—from people who wanted God's will as much as he did.

Disciples at Tyre

Luke tells us what happened there:

> After looking up the disciples, we stayed there seven days; and they kept telling Paul through the Spirit not to set foot in Jerusalem. (v. 4)

"They *kept* telling Paul." Apparently, the Apostle endured a continuous barrage of, "Your life is in danger; don't go to Jerusalem!" These weren't just frivolous opinions, for Luke says that they kept telling him "through the Spirit." For this reason, some commentators say that the Spirit was using these disciples to tell him not to go and that Paul made a mistake by stubbornly going to Jerusalem anyway.[2]

More likely, the Spirit was merely predicting what would happen to Paul in Jerusalem, but the disciples were misinterpreting those predictions as prohibitions. "Perhaps," John Stott asserts, "Luke's statement is a condensed way of saying that the warning was divine while the urging was human."[3]

Sometimes people think they know God's will for our lives, and they tell us in definite terms that we are going in the wrong direction. They may even express their opinion in their prayers as we listen. As the people prayed for Paul when he left town, this kind of "Lord-help-him-see-the-light" prayer may have been on their lips.

> When it came about that our days there were ended, we departed and started on our journey, while they all, with wives and children, escorted us until we were out of the city. And after kneeling down on the beach and praying, we said farewell to one another. Then we went on board the ship, and they returned home again. (vv. 5–6)

Pressured by these well-intentioned believers to change his mind

2. See Ray Stedman, *Acts 21–28: Triumphs of the Body* (Santa Ana, Calif.: Vision House Publishers, 1981), pp. 7–23.

3. John Stott, *The Spirit, the Church, and the World: The Message of Acts* (Downers Grove, Ill.: InterVarsity Press, 1990), p. 333.

about Jerusalem, Paul was probably relieved to be on his way again. But that relief would not last long, for soon other people would be giving him their opinions as well.

Prophet Named Agabus

Having weighed anchor at Tyre, Paul's ship sailed for Ptolemais and then Caesarea (vv. 7–8a). Here the group lodged at "the house of Philip the evangelist" (v. 8b).[4]

> Now this man had four virgin daughters who were prophetesses. And as we were staying there for some days, a certain prophet named Agabus came down from Judea. And coming to us, he took Paul's belt and bound his own feet and hands, and said, "This is what the Holy Spirit says: 'In this way the Jews at Jerusalem will bind the man who owns this belt and deliver him into the hands of the Gentiles.'" (vv. 9–11)

The prophet gave a gripping illustration of Paul's fate—so gripping that everyone present, including Luke, began giving Paul advice.

Dr. Luke and Others

> When we had heard this, we as well as the local residents began begging him not to go up to Jerusalem. (v. 12)

The disciples at Tyre had heaped plenty of advice on Paul, but now piling it on even thicker were his closest friends and fellow ministers. With tears, they were begging him, "Please don't go to Jerusalem—we need you, Paul! How can you lead the church in prison, bound by chains? Don't go!"

Not one person said to him, "Hang in there, Paul. You obey God's plan for your life, and I'll stand with you." The pressure to acquiesce must have been intense. But reverberating through his mind was the thought he had expressed in his letter to the Galatians: "If I were still trying to please men, I would not be a bond-servant of Christ" (Gal. 1:10b).

---

4. This Philip is the same Philip who was one of the first seven deacons in Jerusalem and who later preached the gospel to the Samaritans and to the Ethiopian eunuch (see Acts 6:5 and 8:4–13, 26–40).

He could not change his mind just to please these people. So after quieting them, he responded,

> What are you doing, weeping and breaking my heart? For I am ready not only to be bound, but even to die at Jerusalem for the name of the Lord Jesus. (Acts 21:13)

But weren't Paul's friends merely looking out for his safety and the church's well-being? Maybe so, but while they were looking out for Paul's good, the church's good, and their own good, they were forgetting about God's good. Paul's ministry in Jerusalem would bring the highest glory to God, even if it meant death for the beloved Apostle.

With a tone of resignation, the people in Caesarea relented and Luke completed the account, recording Paul's quick trip to Jerusalem.

> Since he would not be persuaded, we fell silent, remarking, "The will of the Lord be done!" And after these days we got ready and started on our way up to Jerusalem. And some of the disciples from Caesarea also came with us, taking us to Mnason of Cyprus, a disciple of long standing with whom we were to lodge. And when we had come to Jerusalem, the brethren received us gladly. (vv. 14–17)

With his arrival in the holy city, Paul's third missionary journey comes to a close. In the events to follow, the prophecies of his bondage and imprisonment will be fulfilled, as well as his dream to someday proclaim Christ in Rome. In the end, as we'll see in the chapters to come, Christ will be glorified by Paul's unswerving determination to proclaim His name in Jerusalem.

Enduring Principles concerning Others' Advice

By learning from Paul's struggle with his advisors, we can hammer out three shields of truth to protect us in this whole realm of giving and receiving counsel.

First, *if you seek advice, be discerning.* Sometimes counselors are essential. Like in a sports event, we need the advice of a wiser coach, who can see the action in our lives from an objective vantage point. However, as J. Grant Howard cautions,

> Be careful—go to the right sidelines! Get your counsel

and advice from those on *your* team. And when you get to your sidelines, go to the coach, not to the water boy. . . . As for time-outs—they are unlimited. Call one whenever you need one. One other point: Go while the game is still in progress. For example, a man who knows things are not going well in his marriage but is convinced he can handle it by himself may discover that when he finally goes to the sidelines for help, the game is over and it is too late. Time has run out.[5]

Second, *if you give advice, be wise.* Wise counseling always begins with attentive listening. Try to fit yourself into the other person's shoes to understand your friend's perspective; then step away and take a look at him or her from God's viewpoint. Of course, in order to know His viewpoint, you must be acquainted with His Book, and that is your greatest source of wisdom. Howard again helps us with this point:

> When we give Word-oriented counsel, it will be instructive. When we give experience-centered counsel, it may be nothing more than opinion. Our personal attitudes, opinions, and biases always need to be related to the Word before we prescribe them as the right medicine for others.[6]

Third, *if you decide against the advice, be careful.* In Proverbs we read,

> The mind of man plans his way,
> But the Lord directs his steps. (16:9)

Sometimes with the help of an advisor you make plans to go one direction, when suddenly, maybe because a moral principle is at stake, you sense the Lord leading you the opposite way. He's directing your steps according to His Word, and, although your actions may be confusing to others, you have to follow Him.

Think of Paul, who resisted the powerful influence of his closest companions in order to walk Christ's narrow road. Remember, he

5. J. Grant Howard, Jr., *Knowing God's Will—and Doing It!* (Grand Rapids, Mich.: Zondervan Publishing House, 1976), pp. 65–66.

6. Howard, *Knowing God's Will—and Doing It!*, p. 66.

didn't make that decision without considering its consequences. As we receive advice, we must also carefully weigh the consequences. What will happen if we follow that advice? Will taking the smooth path bring as much glory to Christ as taking the rocky way? What does God's Word say will happen if we follow that advice? What is the Spirit's inner prompting telling us?

The answers to these questions are not always black and white. Determining God's will can be complicated. But through the process, let Paul's words of commitment to Christ undergird your thinking:

> I am ready not only to be bound, but even to die
> . . . for the name of the Lord Jesus. (21:13b)

Then, whatever the outcome, you'll have peace.

🌲 Living Insights

Maybe you are wrestling with a problem or a tough decision right now. Are you considering seeking advice? If so, let's take a closer look at J. Grant Howard's recommendations, which we quoted earlier.

First, he encourages us to go to the right sidelines. This may sound obvious, but how often do we seek counsel from the wrong team? Bookstore shelves are lined with worldly advice on how to find happiness by pleasing ourselves. Television, radio, and the movies preach that same message. But by listening to these secular counselors, we are sure to miss God's will. If your advisors have come from the world, where can you find godly advice?

_____

_____

Second, talk to the coach, not the water boy. In other words, we may be seeking counsel in the right place—a church, Christian bookstore, or a Christian counseling practice—but even still must be careful to consult the right person or resource. As you consider your problem or decision, determine who is the person most qualified to advise you in that area. If you're not sure, how can you find out which person to consult or book to read?

_____

Third, take a time-out. In our hurried, beat-the-yellow-light way of living, taking time out is difficult. However, without doing so, we'll find that knowing God's will is impossible. Right now, carve out some space in your schedule to pray, meditate on Scripture, and select appropriate counsel.

Fourth, ask for advice during the game. Don't put off making the decision or solving the problem. Deal with it now, while you can. Make that phone call, read that book, schedule that appointment, take that time-out. Your future may depend on it.

 *Living Insights* STUDY TWO

How easy it would have been for Paul to rationalize not going to Jerusalem. "My friends need me. I can preach the gospel better as a free man. I think I'll stay away from Jerusalem."

Had he made that decision, no one would have criticized him. "Good choice, Paul," they would have said, shaking his hand and patting him on the back.

But had he made that decision, regret and disappointment would have wreaked havoc in his soul. A foreigner called compromise would have invaded his heart and eaten away his zeal for the Lord. He couldn't allow that to happen—he *had* to go to Jerusalem.

Has a commitment to Christ so consumed your spirit that compromise feels like a foreign invader? Or has rationalization made compromise a comfortable houseguest? If so, then remove any self-serving motives in your heart. Resensitize your conscience. And renew your passion to obey Christ, regardless of the consequences.

71

Chapter 9

WHEN MISUNDERSTANDING TAKES CONTROL

Acts 21:17–39

To be great is to be misunderstood,"[1] wrote Ralph Waldo Emerson, and the Scriptures agree. Think of all the great Bible characters who were misunderstood. There was Noah the ark-builder whom the people labeled crazy and David the giant-killer whom King Saul deemed overly ambitious. There was impulsive Moses to whom the Hebrew said, "Are you intending to kill me, as you killed the Egyptian?" (Exod. 2:14b) And visionary Joseph of whom his brothers commented disdainfully, "Here comes this dreamer!" (Gen. 37:19).

Certainly, great people are misunderstood. "This is a part of the penalty for greatness," concurred Elbert Hubbard, a contemporary of Emerson. However, he adds a significant qualifier:

> It is no proof of greatness. The final proof of greatness lies in being able to endure [criticism] without resentment.[2]

Ultimately, then, our reaction to misunderstanding says much more about our character than whatever action triggered it. Through the course of our journeys with Paul, we've seen him react to criticism with a grace and forbearance that illustrates his greatness. The supreme test, however, will come in Jerusalem at the end of his third and final missionary journey.

Journey's End: A Pleasant Reunion

Initially, Paul's arrival in Jerusalem meets with approval and appreciation. Luke, a member of Paul's traveling party, comments, "the brethren received us gladly" (Acts 21:17b). Then the next day, anxious to tell them about his most recent exploits,

---

1. Ralph Waldo Emerson, as quoted in *Bartlett's Familiar Quotations*, 15th ed. rev. and enl., ed. Emily Morison Beck (Boston, Mass.: Little, Brown, and Co., 1980), p. 497.

2. Elbert Hubbard II, ed., *Selected Writings of Elbert Hubbard*, (East Aurora, N.Y.: The Roycrofters, 1922), p. 58.

Paul went in with us to James, and all the elders were present. And after he had greeted them, he began to relate one by one the things which God had done among the Gentiles through his ministry. And when they heard it they began glorifying God; and they said to him, "You see, brother, how many thousands there are among the Jews of those who have believed, and they are all zealous for the Law." (vv. 18–20)

James and the elders praised God for Paul's ministry, but in their response, they shifted the focus from Gentiles to Jews. The reason for this shift becomes apparent in what they say next.

Verbal Misinterpretation: A Wrong Report

Foremost on the minds of these leaders is a rumor about Paul that has been spreading among Jewish Christians in the Jerusalem church.

What Was Being Said?

These Jerusalem believers had kept the Law before believing in Christ, and they had continued following it afterwards. They had circumcised their children, observed the Sabbath and the religious feasts, and maintained their strict dietary code. About them, the leaders of the church say to Paul,

"they have been told about you, that you are teaching all the Jews who are among the Gentiles to forsake Moses, telling them not to circumcise their children nor to walk according to the customs." (v. 21)

Of course, this accusation was unfounded. He had told the Gentiles that they did not have to become Jews to be saved, and the Jerusalem Council had backed that teaching (see 15:19–20 and 21:25). However, he had never barred the Jews from continuing their religious traditions after salvation. In fact, he was particularly sensitive to the Jewish believers, insisting that half-Jewish Timothy be circumcised so as not to offend them (16:1–3).

Even so, these Jewish Christians had been told that Paul was teaching against the Law of Moses . . . *they had been told!* Who told them? What was the evidence? Where were the witnesses? The accusations were based solely on hearsay and gossip.

Swarming insinuations infested the church like bees buzzing here and there among the believers. "My cousin's sister was in Corinth, and she said . . ." "Shameful!" "How can Paul call himself a Jew?" "He's gone too far now!" "Did you hear the latest about Paul . . . ?"

When Paul became aware of this prattle, he could have shot back with a fiery defense. He had been misunderstood; these accusations were unfair; these people didn't know what they were talking about! Instead, he exemplifies his great character by simply listening as the leaders formulate a plan to challenge the church's misconceptions.

What Should Be Done?

"What, then, is to be done?" they ask each other, as they consider how to convince the Jewish believers of Paul's integrity. "They will certainly hear that you have come. Therefore

> do this that we tell you. We have four men who are under a vow; take them and purify yourself along with them, and pay their expenses in order that they may shave their heads; and all will know that there is nothing to the things which they have been told about you, but that you yourself also walk orderly, keeping the Law. But concerning the Gentiles who have believed, we wrote, having decided that they should abstain from meat sacrificed to idols and from blood and from what is strangled and from fornication." (21:22–25)

According to commentator Everett F. Harrison, the four men were poor and, without a benefactor, could not complete their Nazirite vow. So the church leaders suggested that Paul identify himself with them,

> assuming the expenses incident to the fulfillment of the vow, which included the offering of sacrifices. The hair, probably intended to symbolize the life of the individual, was shaved off and burned as an offering (Num. 6:18).[3]

3. Everett F. Harrison, *Interpreting Acts: The Expanding Church* (Grand Rapids, Mich.: Zondervan Publishing House, Academie Books, 1986), p. 345.

By recommending that Paul participate in this custom, the elders hoped he could demonstrate his respect for the Jewish believers and, by his actions, silence the rumors. Paul agreed to the plan, living out his earlier words to the Corinthians:

> For though I am free from all men, I have made myself a slave to all, that I might win the more. And to the Jews I became as a Jew, that I might win Jews; to those who are under the Law, as under the Law, though not being myself under the Law, that I might win those who are under the Law. (1 Cor. 9:19–20)

So, the next day, Paul

> took the men . . . purifying himself along with them, went into the temple, giving notice of the completion of the days of purification, until the sacrifice was offered for each one of them. (Acts 21:26)

As Paul is dousing the flames of false accusation among the Christian Jews, a group of non-Christian Jews begin lighting more fires while his back is turned.

Physical Mistreatment: A Violent Scene

> When the seven days were almost over, the Jews from Asia, upon seeing him in the temple, began to stir up all the multitude and laid hands on him. (v. 27)

These Asian Jews had been seeing their own following dwindle as thousands of their fellows from Derbe to Ephesus were believing in Christ. Now filled with resentment, they long for the opportunity to get rid of Paul. That chance has come, for Paul is on their turf, surrounded by the most zealous Jews in the world. Let's read on to discover their strategy.

Exaggeration

Their first tactic is to exaggerate the truth. Having seized Paul, they display him before the crowd and shout,

> "Men of Israel, come to our aid! This is the man who preaches to all men everywhere against our people, and the Law, and this place." (v. 28a)

None of these accusations are based on evidence, yet temple

Jews swallow the lies whole. Their emotions churn and fume, and their imaginations run wild as their misunderstanding of Paul grows.

Suspicion

Aggravating the mob's suspicion of the Apostle, his accusers rave on:

> "He has even brought Greeks into the temple and has defiled this holy place." For they had previously seen Trophimus the Ephesian in the city with him, and they supposed that Paul had brought him into the temple. (v. 28b–29)

They *supposed* that Paul had brought Trophimus into the temple. Had they actually *seen* him do it? No. They merely suspected that he had, because Trophimus was his friend. That's called basing a charge on circumstantial evidence, and such evidence shouldn't be grounds for conviction . . . it shouldn't be, but it was.

Overreaction

Exaggeration had led to suspicion, and now suspicion almost leads to murder. Because of the slanderous allegations,

> all the city was aroused, and the people rushed together; and taking hold of Paul, they dragged him out of the temple; and immediately the doors were shut. And while they were seeking to kill him, a report came up to the commander of the Roman cohort that all Jerusalem was in confusion. And at once he took along some soldiers and centurions, and ran down to them; and when they saw the commander and the soldiers, they stopped beating Paul. (vv. 30–32)

Slam! The doors, like the people's hearts, shut tight as the crowd drives Paul out of the temple to an area where they can vent their rage. Like a frenzied pack of wolves surrounding a rabbit, they begin tearing into Paul. Only the Roman soldiers are able to stop the madness.[4]

---

4. Rome did not tolerate civil unrest in its conquered regions. A riot such as this one was a sign that the commanders lacked control, and they would have been speedily punished.

Identity Mistaken: An Embarrassing Moment

How ironic—God using a Gentile commander to rescue the Apostle. With the crowd at arm's length, this man orders Paul to be chained and begins asking questions (v. 33).

Inquisition

Who is this man? What has he done?

> Among the crowd some were shouting one thing and some another, and when he could not find out the facts on account of the uproar, he ordered him to be brought into the barracks. And when he got to the stairs, it so happened that he was carried by the soldiers because of the violence of the mob; for the multitude of the people kept following behind, crying out, "Away with him!" (vv. 34–36)

These raging people must have reminded Paul of those who had chanted "Crucify Him! Crucify Him!" at Jesus. Unlike Pilate, though, this Roman commander protected Paul, ordering the soldiers to carry him on their shoulders, just above the clawing of the rabid mob.

Identity

Having heard only a chaotic garble of shouts from the people, the commander still was curious about this man's identity. He thought he knew who he might be, but

> as Paul was about to be brought into the barracks, he said to the commander, "May I say something to you?" And he said, "Do you know Greek? Then you are not the Egyptian who some time ago stirred up a revolt and led the four thousand men of the Assassins out into the wilderness?"[5] But Paul said, "I am a Jew of Tarsus in Cilicia, a citizen of no insignificant city; and I beg you, allow me to speak to the people." (vv. 37–39)

---

5. The Assassins were men "armed with short daggers (sicai) under their cloaks, [who] mingled with the crowd, struck down their opponents, then pretended to call for help." Fritz Rienecker, *A Linguistic Key to the Greek New Testament* (Grand Rapids, Mich.: Zondervan Publishing House, Regency Reference Library, 1980), p. 323.

77

The commander had thought Paul was someone else—an Egyptian who, according to commentator Fritz Rienecker,

> was a Jew who proclaimed himself as a prophet. He gathered a large following intending to lead them to the Mount of Olives promising that at his command the walls of Jerusalem would collapse. His force was attacked by Felix but the Egyptian himself escaped.[6]

The Jews believed Paul to be a blasphemous teacher; now the Romans think he is a dangerous Egyptian brigand! It is amazing how misunderstandings can multiply.

Despite the ridiculous allegations, though, Paul reacts calmly: "Allow me to speak to the people." His trust in Christ soothes any fears or frustrations, and he is able to face his enemies with open arms and an open heart.

In our next chapter, we'll examine Paul's words to the people; for now, let's reflect on what we can learn from his reactions so far.

Application

Paul's experience can teach us three facts about misunderstanding: the reality of it is inescapable, the reason for it is often unpredictable, and our reaction to it can be questionable. In other words, even when we have the best of intentions, our words and actions can and often will be misunderstood—it's inevitable. And the source of the misunderstanding is something we can never fully anticipate. But when it comes, our reaction to it will illumine the truth about our character.

We might be tempted to put on a martyr's sackcloth and sulk, or to pull out our battle fatigues and prepare for war. But the right response is to face our accusers with a loving heart—an option that is only possible if we have cast ourselves into the nail-scarred hands of Christ, who knows above all others what it is like to be misunderstood.

6. Rienecker, *A Linguistic Key to the Greek New Testament*, p. 323.

78

The local church is one of Satan's favorite seedbeds for growing a weedy crop of misunderstandings. He tills our thoughts like soil, mixing in a shovelful of good intentions, a bagful of prejudice, and a few pellets of pride. Then he scatters an accusing word here, an inflamatory comment there, and waits for them to germinate.

◆

"I think we should pray for the pastor's son Kenny," Doug says to his wife, June. "At the church picnic, I forgot the matches to start the barbecue, and as I was asking around, Kenny said he had some. Now, what would a seventeen-year-old boy be doing with a book of matches, unless . . ."

"He smokes?" June finishes the accusation.

"It may be nothing, I know, but when I was a kid, only the smokers carried matches."

Next day . . .

June is talking on the phone. "Yes . . . hmm . . . I can believe it. I've always thought Kenny's car is a bit flashy, and you say Georgene thought she heard him screeching out of the school parking lot? You know, Doug thinks he's smoking too. I wonder what his home life is like?"

Two months later . . .

"I feel that we, as the elder board, ought to do something," Doug says somberly. "I don't like it any more than you do, but if the pastor's son is smoking marijuana, drag racing down the boulevard, and rebelling against his parents, what does that say about his father? If a man can't control his own family, how can he lead the church? The pastor's on vacation until next week. Now is the perfect time to call a church meeting."

◆

From matches to marijuana, from hearsay to fact, misunderstandings in this story grew into a tangled jungle of false accusations. Would you say that your church is a fertile seedbed for unfounded conclusions and gossip? Have you started or passed along a rumor lately? If so, how can you pull it out by the roots before it grows out of control?

_____

_____

Misunderstandings can strangle a church. Instead of accusations, plant a crop of encouraging words, and watch your church flower.

🌲 *Living Insights*
 STUDY TWO

When misunderstanding cast a shadow on Paul's life, how did he react?

1. He didn't retaliate, but took positive steps to clear up the misunderstanding.

2. When he became aware of the misunderstandings, he didn't allow his emotions to blur his judgment; rather, he listened and agreed to a plan to correct the people's thinking.

3. His attitude was not vindictive, but loving. He wanted to help the people resolve their anger and trust Christ as he had done.

4. He didn't run from his accusers; instead, he faced them directly.

5. Whatever the outcome, he had a settled confidence that God was in control.

Have you been misunderstood lately? If so, how can Paul's example guide your reactions? For each of the above points, write down how you can follow his model in your own situation.

1. _____

2. _____

3. _____

4. _____

5. _____

Chapter 10

AN UNANSWERABLE ARGUMENT

Acts 21:40–22:30

H e made the Pharisees mad just by looking at them. In their rigid world, blind men were blind because they were sinners. And people like him didn't get second chances.

But what perturbed them most was *how* he had gained his sight. According to him,

> "The man who is called Jesus made clay, and anointed my eyes, and said to me, 'Go to Siloam, and wash'; so I went away and washed, and I received sight." (John 9:11)

But this was the Sabbath! Everyone knew that making clay on the Sabbath was sinful. Therefore, Jesus was a sinner, and sinners couldn't perform miracles. This had to be some kind of trick!

"Give glory to God," they said, egging him to confess. "We know that this man [Jesus] is a sinner" (v. 24b). But he could only answer,

> "Whether He is a sinner, I do not know; one thing I do know, that, whereas I was blind, now I see." (v. 25)

He blinked and just looked at them again—that really made them mad.

The Jewish leaders in Jesus' day were responding in frustration to an unanswerable argument. The healed man's testimony contained personal experience plus irrefutable facts, proving beyond doubt that Jesus was the Son of God. Ironically, the Pharisees, who had healthy eyes, couldn't see that truth.

In our passage in Acts, Paul is standing before another spiritually blind group at the temple. He is about to tell them how he used to be like them, but now sees. He will not use heavy theology or brilliant logic; like the blind man in Jesus' day, the argument of his changed life will be unanswerable.

Exposition of Acts 22

The events surrounding Paul's first defense of the faith can be divided into four sections.[1] The first section concerns the presentation itself.

Speaking before the Jews

At the stairs leading into the military barracks, the Apostle asks the Roman commander if he can speak to the hostile crowd that is still calling out for his death (21:35–39).

> And when he had given him permission, Paul, standing on the stairs, motioned to the people with his hand; and when there was a great hush, he spoke to them in the Hebrew dialect, saying,
> "Brethren and fathers, hear my defense which I now offer to you."
> And when they heard that he was addressing them in the Hebrew dialect, they became even more quiet. (Acts 21:40–22:2)

The Hebrew dialect Paul used was Aramaic, the language of the Jews in Palestine. By using their tongue and calling them "brethren and fathers," he was identifying with the people—the first door anyone must open in ministering to others. Continuing his efforts to win a hearing among them, Paul gives further credentials:

> "I am a Jew, born in Tarsus of Cilicia, but brought up in this city, educated under Gamaliel, strictly according to the law of our fathers, being zealous for God, just as you all are today. And I persecuted this Way to the death, binding and putting both men and women into prisons, as also the high priest and all the Council of the elders can testify. From them I also received letters to the brethren, and started off for Damascus in order to bring even those who were there to Jerusalem as prisoners to be punished." (22:3–5)

Paul's heritage, his training under the highly respected Gamaliel, and his energetic zeal to keep the Law and expunge Christianity give him credibility with his audience. Using plain language—not fancy theology or religious jargon—he is making himself real to

---

1. For an overview of Paul's six defenses of the faith in Acts 22–26, see the Digging Deeper at the end of this chapter.

them, which opens the next door: sharing his salvation experience.

> "And it came about that as I was on my way, approaching Damascus about noontime, a very bright light suddenly flashed from heaven all around me, and I fell to the ground and heard a voice saying to me, 'Saul, Saul, why are you persecuting Me?' And I answered, 'Who art Thou, Lord?' And He said to me, 'I am Jesus the Nazarene, whom you are persecuting.'" (vv. 6–8)

This is the crucial point in Paul's presentation, for now the mob has to come to terms with the fact that Jesus Christ is alive. They thought they had nailed Him to the cross and shut Him in the tomb, but Paul is saying, "No, I saw Him alive and He changed my life."

As the people listen intently, he continues his story about how the light blinded him and the Voice told him to go on to Damascus (vv. 9–11). Having been led by the hand to the city, he waited there until Ananias came to him, healed his eyes, and gave him his new commission (vv. 14–16). Then Paul relates a part of his story we didn't hear about in Luke's account of his conversion.

> "And it came about when I returned to Jerusalem and was praying in the temple, that I fell into a trance, and I saw Him saying to me, 'Make haste, and get out of Jerusalem quickly, because they will not accept your testimony about Me.' And I said, 'Lord, they themselves understand that in one synagogue after another I used to imprison and beat those who believed in Thee. And when the blood of Thy witness Stephen was being shed, I also was standing by approving, and watching out for the cloaks of those who were slaying him.'" (vv. 17–20)

That was what Paul did in his old life: imprison, beat, approve of the stonings of Christians. But the Lord divinely interrupted that course and changed its direction. The most radical shift in Paul's thinking occurred when God explained to him His new plan for the world. So Paul next recounts to his Jewish listeners what the Lord told him:

> "And He said to me, 'Go! For I will send you far away to the Gentiles.'" (v. 21)

Gentiles?! Red lights flash and sirens buzz immediately in the minds of Paul's zealously Jewish audience. And although Paul wasn't quite finished with what he wanted to say, in their minds he was through.

Reaction of the Jews

> They listened to him up to this statement, and then they raised their voices and said, "Away with such a fellow from the earth, for he should not be allowed to live!" And . . . they were crying out and throwing off their cloaks and tossing dust into the air. (vv. 22–23)

The possibility that God could relate directly to the Gentiles through Christ greatly offended them. In their way of thinking, all others in the world—except God's chosen Jews—were unworthy of God's offer of salvation. Theirs was the ultimate prejudice.

Enraged, this crowd would have torn Paul apart had it not been for the soldiers protecting him. Yet, in the Jews' reaction to Paul's words, notice what was absent: they shouted, they stamped, they threw dust in the air—but no one countered Paul's defense! His argument was unanswerable. He had presented a subjective account of his changed life and had backed it up with the objective reality of Jesus Christ risen from the dead. In addition, that same risen Christ had changed thousands of other people who, along with Paul, were turning the world upside down. All this evidence was too much for them to handle.

And when the Roman commander saw them become violent, he reacted quickly to silence the riot.

Standing before the Romans

Now the Greek-speaking commander had not understood a word Paul had said. In his mind, something criminal must have been behind the tumult, so he

> ordered him to be brought into the barracks, stating that he should be examined by scourging so that he might find out the reason why they were shouting against him that way. (v. 24)

Why would the commander order scourging? "This was not a punishment," explains William Barclay.

It was simply the most effective way of extracting either the truth or a confession. The scourge was a leather whip studded at intervals with sharp pieces of bone and lead. Few men survived it in their right senses and many died under it.[2]

However, there was a small problem with this method, which Paul wasted no time in bringing to their attention.

> When they stretched him out with thongs, Paul said to the centurion who was standing by, "Is it lawful for you to scourge a man who is a Roman and un-condemned?" And when the centurion heard this, he went to the commander and told him, saying, "What are you about to do? For this man is a Ro-man." And the commander came and said to him, "Tell me, are you a Roman?" And he said, "Yes." And the commander answered, "I acquired this citi-zenship with a large sum of money." And Paul said, "But I was actually born a citizen." Therefore those who were about to examine him immediately let go of him; and the commander also was afraid when he found out that he was a Roman, and because he had put him in chains. (vv. 25–29)

Knowing that it is illegal for a Roman citizen to be bound and beaten, probably to death, Paul stops the soldiers in their tracks. For although Christ had called him to suffer for His name, that calling did not include *needless* suffering. And Paul knew that his task wasn't completed yet; he must still go to Rome. So he wisely guarded his life. As a result, since the commander couldn't whip the answers out of him, he turned him loose again to his own people.

Release to the Council

> On the next day, wishing to know for certain why he had been accused by the Jews, he released him and ordered the chief priests and all the Council to assemble, and brought Paul down and set him before them. (v. 30)

2. William Barclay, *The Acts of the Apostles*, rev. ed., The Daily Study Bible Series (Phila-delphia, Pa.: Westminster Press, 1976), p. 163.

We'll reserve Paul's address to the Sanhedrin for the following chapter. For now, let's pause for a moment to review a couple of truths from this passage.

Application

First, from Paul we learn that experience alone is questionable, but a testimony based on facts is unanswerable. The focus of our witnessing should be Jesus Christ—His life, death, and resurrection. These are the bones and muscle of our testimony, and our personal experience is the flesh with which our hearers identify. Experience without facts removes the substance of our claim, resulting in a defense of Christianity that can be easily struck down.

Second, we also learn that humility is one thing, but indignity is something else entirely. When the soldiers were preparing Paul for scourging, he could have thought, "This suffering is God's will; I shouldn't defend myself." But he knew that being needlessly victimized is not the same as humbly suffering for Christ. The scourgings of a battered wife, an abused employee, or a molested child are not examples of biblical submission. There is a time to claim our rights as citizens of God's kingdom and defend ourselves. We'll explore this point more closely in the following Living Insight.

Living Insights   STUDY ONE

Indignities tolerated in the name of submission are the scourges of the human spirit—they violate a person's worth, sense of honor, and self-esteem. They may be verbal or nonverbal, subtle or outright—against a child, spouse, friend, or coworker.

Have you been victimized by a wrongful demand for submission that assaulted your dignity? In what way?

_____

_____

_____

How have you tried to cope with this?

_____

_____

If you've been abused, you don't need to silently endure it any longer. Christ never meant biblical submission to be an excuse for abuse. As Richard Foster explains:

> Of all the Spiritual Disciplines none has been more abused than the Discipline of submission. . . . Nothing in religion has done more to manipulate and destroy people than a deficient teaching on submission. . . .
> The limits of the Discipline of submission are at the points at which it becomes destructive. It then becomes a denial of the law of love as taught by Jesus and is an affront to genuine biblical submission.
> . . . Therefore we must work our way through this Discipline with great care and discernment in order to insure that we are the ministers of life, not death.[3]

In the same way that Paul had rights as a Roman citizen, you have rights as a citizen of God's kingdom—the rights of dignity, self-respect, and honor. If you are being abused, or someone else in your home is, take the first step toward freedom by calling it what it is. Don't be afraid to stop denying it; denial is not your friend— it's another attacker.

For further help, we recommend the following resources:

Allender, Dan B. *The Wounded Heart*. Colorado Springs, Colo.: NavPress, 1990.

Alsdurf, James and Phyllis. *Battered into Submission: The Tragedy of Wife Abuse in the Christian Home*. Downers Grove, Ill.: Inter-Varsity Press, 1989.

Dobson, James C. *Love Must Be Tough*. Waco, Tex.: Word Books, 1983.

---

3. Richard J. Foster, *Celebration of Discipline* (San Francisco, Calif.: Harper and Row, Publishers, 1978), pp. 96, 105.

Strom, Kay Marshall. *Helping Women in Crisis*. Grand Rapids, Mich.: Zondervan Publishing House, Ministry Resources Library, 1986.

Living Insights

If our testimony is just "Jesus makes me feel good," then our argument for Christianity is easily answered: "That's fine for you, but it's not for me." How can we present an unanswerable argument for our faith?

Before he spoke of Christ, Paul began his argument by identifying with his listeners and describing portions of his life (see Acts 22:3–5). Consider a few people with whom you would like to share your testimony. How could you describe your life in a way they could relate to?

Paul then explained his encounter with Christ (see vv. 6–11). Describe the moment when Christ confronted you on your Damascus road.

In Damascus, Ananias' prophecy verified Paul's vision (see vv. 12–16). What biblical facts validate your experience? If you need some help remembering, the following verses might supply you with the facts you need. Add any other significant passages of your own to the list.

- Jesus is God in the flesh. (Col. 2:9)
- Jesus lived a sinless life. (Heb. 4:15)
- My sin condemns me to death. (Rom. 6:23)
- Jesus died on the cross in my place. (Rom. 5:8)
- Jesus' resurrection guarantees my new life with Him. (Rom. 6:4–5)

Your significant verses:

_____

Paul next explained how he received forgiveness by "calling on His name" or trusting Christ (Acts 22:16). Explain how you trusted Christ.

_____

_____

_____

Finally, Paul told of his mission in life after he became a Christian (see vv. 18–21). In what direction has Christ pointed you?

_____

_____

_____

Paul's audience reacted violently to his testimony (vv. 22–23). Your listeners, too, may scoff at your testimony, but they will not be able to deny the facts. Hopefully, they will accept them—then they _would_ have an answer for your argument . . . "I believe."

Digging Deeper

Between his arrest in Jerusalem (Acts 21:27–39) and his departure for Rome (Acts 27:1–2), the apostle Paul delivered six separate speeches in defense of his faith in Jesus Christ. Following is a chart with each defense.

Survey of Six Defenses of the Faith
Acts 22–26

SCRIPTURE	LOCATION	AUDIENCE	RESULT
Acts 22:1–30	Jerusalem	Jewish populace and Roman commander	Fear upon hearing of Paul's Roman citizenship (22:29). Released Paul to stand before the Jewish Council.
Acts 23:1–10	Jerusalem	Sanhedrin	Dissension in ranks between Pharisees and Sadducees. Threat of bodily harm. Paul protected. Plans to murder Paul established (23:12).
Acts 24:10–23	Caesarea (governor's residence) *"Herod's Praetorium"*	Felix Governor of Judea A.D. 52–60	Kindly disposed toward Paul. Delays decision. Allows limited freedom, visitors. Awaits another audience.
Acts 24:24–27	Caesarea	Felix and Drusilla Second appearance	Felix obviously shaken. Again, delays decision. Sends Paul back to prison. Periodic dialogues occur.
Acts 25:8–12	Caesarea *"the tribunal"*	Porcius Festus Governor of Judea A.D. 60–62	Paul found innocent of charges (25:25). Appeal to Caesar granted.
Acts 26:1–32	Caesarea *"the auditorium"*	Festus, Bernice, Agrippa II, large audience (Agrippa ruled parts of Palestine, A.D. 53–70.)	Paul declared mentally incompetent by Festus—"You are out of your mind!"—but harmless. All agreed Paul was innocent. Appeal to Caesar approved, reluctantly.

Chapter 11

WHEN PRESSURE MOUNTS
Acts 23:1–23

In a poem he titled simply "If—," Rudyard Kipling wrote these
lines:

> If you can keep your head when all about you
>   Are losing theirs and blaming it on you;
> If you can trust yourself when all men doubt you,
>   But make allowance for their doubting too;
> If you can wait and not be tired by waiting,
>   Or, being lied about, don't deal in lies,
> Or, being hated, don't give way to hating,
>   And yet don't look too good, nor talk too
>   wise; . . .
>
> If you can talk with crowds and keep your virtue,
>   Or walk with kings—nor lose the common
>   touch;
> If neither foes nor loving friends can hurt you;
>   If all men count with you, but none too much;
> If you can fill the unforgiving minute
>   With sixty seconds' worth of distance run—
> Yours is the Earth and everything that's in it,
>   And—which is more—you'll be a Man, my son! [1]

Many Bible characters epitomized this poet's ideal, among whom
we find the apostle Paul. But even in his exemplary life, Paul sometimes showed signs of stress. In this passage, Luke records one of
those moments in which Paul failed to keep his head when others
were losing theirs.

Paul before the Council

To understand Paul's state of mind, let's recall his recent trou-
bles. So far this week he has been beaten by a mob (Acts 21:27–32),
bound in chains (v. 33), had his death demanded by a group of

---

1. Rudyard Kipling, "If—," in *The World's Best-Loved Poems*, comp. James Gilchrist Lawson
(New York, N.Y.: Harper and Row, Publishers, 1955), pp. 352–53.

zealous Jews (22:1–22), and come within a hairsbreadth of being scourged (vv. 23–29). Now, "wishing to know for certain why he had been accused by the Jews," the Roman commander in charge of Paul

> released him and ordered the chief priests and all the Council to assemble, and brought Paul down and set him before them. (v. 30b)

What a week! And next, having had little sleep, food, or physical care, he stands weary and bruised before the highest Jewish court, the Sanhedrin.[2]

A Description of the Sanhedrin

Paul had been a member of this austere judicial body in his early years and knew all the details about it.[3] It was made up of about seventy men, including the high priest, who wrote laws and made judgments based on their interpretation of the Mosaic Law. And since these men held their positions for life, Paul probably recognized many from his own days on the Council.

He also knew that two main factions divided the Council: the Pharisees, to whom he had belonged, and the Sadducees. The men in his old party were legalistic, like America's Puritans. They also viewed the oral traditions as highly as the written Law and believed in angels, spirits, and the bodily resurrection of the dead. The Sadducees, on the other hand, had no room for oral traditions and were rationalists, rejecting the supernatural altogether—including the hope of a resurrection.

Both factions clung tightly to their traditions—and together to their power. Let's watch how Paul handles himself when he has the chance to speak in person to this group.

A Dialogue among Men

We can imagine Paul, exhausted and in pain, struggling to keep cool as he stands alone before these antagonistic men. His face and

---

2. Throughout Acts, Luke refers to the Sanhedrin simply as "the Council."

3. We assume Paul was a member of the Sanhedrin based on Acts 26:10, where he says, "Not only did I lock up many of the saints in prisons, having received authority from the chief priests, but also when they were being put to death I cast my vote against them" (emphasis added). Only a member of the Sanhedrin could vote.

the inference of his brash opening statement, however, betray his feelings.

> Paul, looking intently at the Council, said, "Brethren, I have lived my life with a perfectly good conscience before God up to this day." (23:1)

He was saying, possibly in a sarcastic tone, "I am not guilty, and you are wrong in judging me." Of course the self-righteous high priest took this as an insult and "commanded those standing beside him to strike him on the mouth" (v. 2).

That did it! After his horrible week, that slap was all the abuse Paul could take. Controlling himself no longer, he suddenly pours out a scalding stream of contempt directly at his enemy.

> "God is going to strike you, you whitewashed wall!⁴
> And do you sit to try me according to the Law, and in violation of the Law order me to be struck?"⁵ (v. 3)

In effect, Paul calls the judge a stinking hypocrite, speaking more out of spite than righteous indignation. He realizes his hotheaded mistake when bystanders respond,

> "Do you revile God's high priest?" And Paul said, "I was not aware, brethren, that he was high priest; for it is written, 'You shall not speak evil of a ruler of your people.'" (vv. 4–5)

How could Paul not have known that the object of his tirade was the high priest? Many scholars believe that Paul had poor eyesight;⁶ maybe he couldn't see him clearly. Or perhaps, as Everett Harrison suggests,

> Paul did not know Ananias personally. He had not had contact with the Sanhedrin for more than twenty years. The high priest may not have been wearing his official robes on this occasion, since he was not ministering in the temple and, in view of

4. Compare this with Jesus' indictment of the religious leaders in Matthew 23:27.

5. The oral tradition the high priest was violating was this: "He who strikes the cheek of an Israelite, strikes, as it were, the glory of God." William Barclay, *The Acts of the Apostles*, rev. ed., The Daily Study Bible Series (Philadelphia, Pa.: Westminster Press, 1976), p. 164.

6. Paul's failing eyesight is alluded to in Galatians 4:15 and 6:11.

the fact that the meeting had been called by Claudius Lysias, may not have been presiding.[7]

Whatever the reason, the damage had been done. In a heated moment, Paul had said the wrong thing to the wrong person, lost his opportunity to receive a fair trial, and, most importantly, blown his chance to explain the gospel. As a result, the situation turns ugly, and Paul now has to think fast just to get out alive. So,

> perceiving that one part were Sadducees and the other Pharisees, Paul began crying out in the Council, "Brethren, I am a Pharisee, a son of Pharisees; I am on trial for the hope and resurrection of the dead!" (v. 6)

This strategic statement polarizes the Council and, for a moment, takes the heat off Paul.

Dissension between Two Groups

With the Sadducees shouting that there is no such thing as resurrection and the Pharisees demanding that there certainly is,

> there arose a great uproar; and some of the scribes of the Pharisaic party stood up and began to argue heatedly, saying, "We find nothing wrong with this man; suppose a spirit or an angel has spoken to him?" And as a great dissension was developing, the commander was afraid Paul would be torn to pieces by them and ordered the troops to go down and take him away from them by force, and bring him into the barracks. (vv. 9–10)

Once again, the commander intervened and saved Paul's skin, something at which he was becoming an expert! He had hoped for a resolution in this case, but only received more fireworks from the volatile Jews.

The Lord with Paul

Back in prison, Paul sits alone, covered in guilt's ashes. Instead

---

7. Everett F. Harrison, *Interpreting Acts: The Expanding Church* (Grand Rapids, Mich.: Zondervan Publishing House, Academie Books, 1986), p. 367.

of bravely carrying the torch of Christ to his former peers, he had overpowered the gospel message with his own explosive anger. Having let down his Lord so badly, how could he go on?

It's then, at just the right moment, that the Lord comes to him.

> But on the night immediately following, the Lord stood at his side and said, "Take courage; for as you have solemnly witnessed to My cause at Jerusalem, so you must witness at Rome also." (v. 11)

With a cool breeze of grace, Jesus blew away the stagnant memories of Paul's failure. How invigorated he must have felt! He was forgiven, restored, and ready to meet any difficulty. Only the grace of God can carve a roadway of peace through a person's wilderness of guilt, course a river of joy through a desert of despair (see Isa. 43:2, 15–16, 18–19).

Paul awakens the next day feeling confident and refreshed. The Jews, however, awake determined to take revenge.

The Jews among Themselves

When daybreak comes, a group of more than forty Jews plot to take Paul's life, conspiring with the chief priests and elders themselves, saying,

> "We have bound ourselves under a solemn oath to taste nothing until we have killed Paul. Now, therefore, you and the Council notify the commander to bring him down to you, as though you were going to determine his case by a more thorough investigation; and we for our part are ready to slay him before he comes near the place." (Acts 23:14b–15)

Again Paul's life is in danger. This time, however, God is not only going to use the mighty Romans to protect His Apostle—He plans to use an unlikely eavesdropper as well.

Paul and the Romans

The conspirators think their plan is a secret,

> but the son of Paul's sister heard of their ambush, and he came and entered the barracks and told Paul. And Paul called one of the centurions to him and

said, "Lead this young man to the commander, for he has something to report to him." So he took him and led him to the commander and said, "Paul the prisoner called me to him and asked me to lead this young man to you since he has something to tell you." And the commander took him by the hand and stepping aside, began to inquire of him privately.

Repeating the plot scheme by scheme, Paul's nephew is then released with the admonition to keep his conversation with the commander confidential (vv. 19b–22). And the commander, getting serious about the murderous Jews,

called to him two of the centurions, and said, "Get two hundred soldiers ready for the third hour of the night to proceed to Caesarea, with seventy horsemen and two hundred spearmen." (v. 23)

Isn't it amazing how God pulled off Paul's deliverance? Just think about all that had to occur:

1. The otherwise unknown nephew just happened to overhear the plot.

2. He somehow entered the heavily guarded barracks to tell Paul.

3. A centurion was willing to take him to the commander.

4. The busy commander listened to him right away and believed him.

5. Then the commander ordered a small army to escort Paul out of town under cover of darkness.

When God makes a promise, He keeps it in grand style!

Application for Today

As Paul rode out of Jerusalem more like a king than a prisoner, he must have been marveling at God's extravagant grace and power. All of us who struggle to keep calm under pressure, who tire of waiting, and who feel hatred's burning coals within need to remember those two words. For they teach us two truths: the *grace* of God can overshadow any guilt within us, and the *power* of God can overcome any plot against us.

Are you wandering in a wilderness of guilt? Are you lost in a desert of despair? Find peace today at the cool springs of God's grace and power.

🌲 *Living Insights*

Imagine Paul in his prison cell after his angry outburst in the Sanhedrin council chamber. Leaning his back against the wall, he sits with his legs drawn up and his head resting on his forearms. He is exhausted but cannot sleep because of the guilt that whips him as hard as any scourging. "I had a once-in-a-lifetime opportunity to preach the gospel to the highest Jewish officials in the world, and I blew it. How stupid I was to lose my temper! 'The Great Apostle'— hardly. 'The Great Failure' is more like it."

Have you ever felt like this? Are you lashing yourself right now because you spoiled a ripe opportunity to share Christ with someone important in your life? What's your situation?

_____

_____

_____

Paul may have thought Christ would be angry at him. But what three examples of grace did Jesus give him instead (Acts 23:11)?

_____

_____

_____

Paul must have been amazed at Jesus' words, particularly this line: "You have solemnly witnessed to My cause at Jerusalem." While Paul only saw his failure, Jesus only saw his successes. Isn't that gracious!

If Christ were to stand beside you in your prison of guilt, what do you think He would say to impart grace to you? If you need some help getting started, turn to Psalm 103:1–13 and listen for His voice in these verses.

_____

_____

_____

_____

🌲 *Living Insights* STUDY TWO

When we feel we've blown it in our efforts to live for Christ, the following words, from a missionary who wrote to author David Seamands, could be ours:

> I know all the answers, all the Scriptures, and can quote the exact chapter and verse. But it is all in my head. The God I serve is never pleased with me and is certainly nothing like the gracious loving God I say I believe in—and tell others about. Why can't I practice what I preach? I feel like a fake.[8]

Seamands contends that these feelings of inadequacy and frustration result partly from viewing our relationship with God more as that of a servant to a master than a child to a loving parent. He elaborates on how these perspectives can affect our feelings toward Him . . . and toward life.

> The servant is accepted and appreciated on the basis of what he does, the child on the basis of who he is.
> The servant starts the day anxious and worried, wondering if his work will really please his master. The child rests in the secure love of his family.
> The servant is accepted because of his workmanship, the son or daughter because of a relationship.
> The servant is accepted because of his productivity and performance. The child belongs because of his position as a person.
> At the end of the day, the servant has peace of

8. David A. Seamands, *Healing Grace* (Wheaton, Ill.: Scripture Press Publications, Victor Books, 1988), pp. 15–16.

mind only if he is sure he has proven his worth by his work. The next morning his anxiety begins again. The child can be secure all day, and know that tomorrow won't change his status.

When a servant fails, his whole position is at stake; he might lose his job. When a child fails, he will be grieved because he has hurt his parents, and he will be corrected and disciplined. But he is not afraid of being thrown out. His basic confidence is in belonging and being loved, and his performance does not change the stability of his position.[9]

Would you say that you relate to God more as a servant to his master than a child to her father? Give some examples of how you fill that role.

_____

_____

_____

Take a moment to read Galatians 4:4–7. Do you think of yourself more in the servant/master relationship? How would changing your perspective to that of the child/father relationship abate your fears and frustrations and help you live within God's grace?

_____

_____

_____

9. Seamands, *Healing Grace*, p. 23.

Chapter 12

BETWEEN THE FRYING PAN AND THE FIRE

Acts 23:23–24:9

There is an appointed time for everything.
And there is a time for every event under
heaven—
>A time to give birth, and a time to die;
>A time to plant, and a time to uproot
>what is planted.
>A time to kill, and a time to heal;
>A time to tear down, and a time to build up.
>A time to weep, and a time to laugh;
>A time to mourn, and a time to dance.
>A time to throw stones, and a time to
>gather stones;
>A time to embrace, and a time to shun
>embracing.
>A time to search, and a time to give up as
>lost;
>A time to keep, and a time to throw away.
>A time to tear apart, and a time to sew to-
>gether;
>A time to be silent, and a time to speak.
(Eccles. 3:1–7)

Paul's life eloquently illustrates the wisdom of these ancient lines. There were times when he planted truth and other times when he uprooted false teaching, times when he tore down sin and times when he built up God's kingdom, times when he wept with people in pain and times when he laughed with them in victory.

There were also times when he spoke forcefully and times when he was noticeably silent. The following passage is about a time of silence in Paul's life when, under attack, he quietly trusted God.

A Brief Review

Misunderstood and falsely accused by the Jews, Paul has recently been the flash point of a riot in Jerusalem, the center of a volatile debate before the Sanhedrin, and the object of a life-threatening conspiracy. Now, escaping to Caesarea by night, the pressure is temporarily off and he is breathing a little easier. But this is only a short respite, for in a sense he is merely jumping from the frying pan of Jerusalem into the fire of Caesarea.

Escape and Arrival

Paul's escape is like none other in his life. Years earlier, he had eluded his enemies by being lowered from a window in a basket (Acts 9:23–25). On another occasion, he was escorted out of town by a group of concerned believers (vv. 29–30). This time, though, Roman soldiers are escorting him to safety—quite a change for this humble missionary! Let's examine more closely what happens to Paul on his flight.

Roman Commander and the Escort

The Roman commander who had ordered Paul's escort went to extraordinary lengths to ensure his safety for the trip. He could have taken care of Paul, his riot-control problem, by looking the other way as the conspirators put an end to him. But instead,

> he called to him two of the centurions, and said, "Get two hundred soldiers ready by the third hour of the night to proceed to Caesarea, with seventy horsemen and two hundred spearmen." They were also to provide mounts to put Paul on and bring him safely to Felix the governor. (23:23–24)

The number of soldiers added up to 470 men—a small army! Why would the Roman commander give such VIP treatment to Paul, a Jew? Perhaps the answer can be found in the proverb,

> When a man's ways are pleasing to the Lord,
> He makes even his enemies to be at peace with
>   him.
> (Prov. 16:7)

The recent melee with the Sanhedrin didn't mean God had abandoned Paul; rather, God was there behind the scenes all along, directing the otherwise Jew-hating Romans to safeguard His servant. In fact, as we'll see, God will be cradling Paul in the palm of His

101

hand no matter what hardships lie waiting around the bend (see Isa. 49:15–16).

One of those hardships will be a trial before Governor Felix in Caesarea. He is the official to whom the Roman commander Claudius Lysias is sending Paul, and Luke even records his letter to the governor, which bears the commander's name.

> "Claudius Lysias, to the most excellent governor Felix, greetings. When this man was arrested by the Jews and was about to be slain by them I came upon them with the troops and rescued him, having learned that he was a Roman.[1] And wanting to ascertain the charge for which they were accusing him, I brought him down to their Council; and I found him to be accused over questions about their Law, but under no accusation deserving death or imprisonment. And when I was informed that there would be a plot against the man, I sent him to you at once, also instructing his accusers to bring charges against him before you." (Acts 23:26–30)

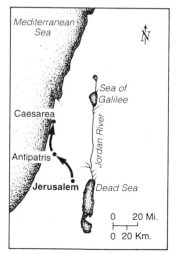

With this letter of introduction, Paul is off to Caesarea and another trial. The entourage travels by night through the hilly, shadowy regions around Jerusalem as far as Antipatris, where the land is flat and open and the danger of ambush left behind. Here half the soldiers return to Jerusalem and the other half accompany Paul the rest of the way to Caesarea[2] (vv. 31–32).

Imprisonment in Caesarea[3]

---

1. Isn't it interesting that Claudius leaves out of his letter how he almost scourged Paul before finding out he was a Roman citizen?

2. Caesarea, built by Herod the Great and named after Augustus Caesar, was the center of government and the Roman military headquarters in Palestine. It is about a sixty-five mile journey from Jerusalem west to Caesarea along the Mediterranean coast.

3. Maps ©1986, 1988 are taken from the *Life Application Bible* ©1988, 1989, 1990, 1991 by Tyndale House Publishers, Inc., Wheaton, IL 60189. Used by permission. All rights reserved. *Life Application* is a trademark of Tyndale House Publishers, Inc.

Governor Felix and Caesarea

And when these had come to Caesarea and delivered the letter to the governor, they also presented
Paul to him. (v. 33)

We can imagine Paul, dusty and travel-worn, chained hand and
foot, yet filled with calm confidence as he stands before Felix. What
kind of man was he facing in the governor's chair? William Barclay
describes this interesting—and treacherous—man.

He had begun life as a slave. His brother, Pallas, was
the favorite of Nero. Through the influence of Pallas,
Felix had risen first to be a freedman and then to be
a governor. He was the first slave in history ever to
become the governor of a Roman province. Tacitus,
the Roman historian, said of him, "He exercised the
prerogatives of a king with the spirit of a slave." . . .
He was completely unscrupulous and was capable of
hiring thugs to murder his own closest supporters. It
was to face a man like that that Paul went to Caesarea.[4]

Ruthless, conniving, and murderous—that was Felix, Paul's
judge! Would he view Paul as a threat? Would he brush him off as
just another fanatic? Or would he thoughtfully listen to his defense?
As Paul stood before him in this pressure-filled moment, many
questions must have raced through his mind. What would Felix do?

The governor examines the letter that was given to him,

and when he had read it, he asked from what province he was; and when he learned that he was from
Cilicia, he said, "I will give you a hearing after your
accusers arrive also," giving orders for him to be kept
in Herod's Praetorium. (vv. 34–35)

Apparently, the Apostle responded to the governor's question
with only one word, "Cilicia." That was all. This was a time to
remain silent, a time for restraint and self-control, for thinking and
praying . . . and trusting God.

---

4. William Barclay, *The Acts of the Apostles*, rev. ed., The Daily Study Bible Series (Philadelphia, Pa.: Westminster Press, 1976), pp. 167–68.

Accusations and Witnesses

Meanwhile, back in Jerusalem, the forty-plus men who had vowed not to eat until Paul was dead are getting mad and hungry! Eventually, they realize their plot has been foiled and Paul is safely away. Probably recanting their oath, they cook up a meal and, at the same time, brew their next plot to dispose of Paul, taking advantage of Felix's wish to hear their side of the story.

Audience with Felix

Finally, after five days of conniving,

> the high priest Ananias came down with some elders, with a certain attorney named Tertullus; and they brought charges to the governor against Paul. (24:1)

Literally, the word describing Tertullus is *orator*. "Such a person," remarks W. E. Vine,

> . . . was hired, as a professional speaker, to make a skilful presentation of a case in court. His training was not legal but rhetorical.[5]

The Jewish leaders wanted a persuader, someone who could tell Felix what he wanted to hear and who could ignite fiery accusations against Paul while clouding the facts. Tertullus was their man.

Charges against Paul

When Tertullus and the religious heavyweights arrive in Caesarea, Paul is summoned to the courtroom. As the trial begins, the hired rhetorician blows a smoke screen of flattery over Felix:

> "Since we have through you attained much peace, and since by your providence reforms are being carried out for this nation, we acknowledge this in every way and everywhere, most excellent Felix, with all thankfulness. But, that I may not weary you any further, I beg you to grant us, by your kindness, a brief hearing." (vv. 2b–4)

Of course, none of that is true. Felix has ruled through corruption and violence, and the Jews hate him. But Tertullus is buttering

5. W. E. Vine, *Vine's Expository Dictionary of Old and New Testament Words* (Old Tappan, N.J.: Fleming H. Revell Co., 1981), vol. 3, p. 144.

him up to believe the accusations he is about to level against Paul.

> "We have found this man a real pest and a fellow who stirs up dissension among all the Jews throughout the world, and a ringleader of the sect of the Nazarenes. And he even tried to desecrate the temple; and then we arrested him. [And we wanted to judge him according to our own Law. But Lysias the commander came along, and with much violence took him out of our hands, ordering his accusers to come before you.] And by examining him yourself concerning all these matters, you will be able to ascertain the things of which we accuse him." And the Jews also joined in the attack, asserting that these things were so. (vv. 5–9)

William Barclay identifies the three main charges in this speech.

> (i) Paul was a fomenter of troubles and a pest. That classed Paul with those insurrectionaries who continually inflamed the inflammable populace into rebellion. Tertullus well knew that the one thing that tolerant Rome would not stand was civil disorder, for any spark might become a flame. . . .
> (ii) Paul was a leader of the sect of the Nazarenes. That coupled Paul with Messianic movements; and the Romans knew what havoc false Messiahs could cause and how they could whip the people into hysterical risings which were only settled at the cost of blood. . . .
> (iii) Paul was a defiler of the Temple. The priests were Sadducees, the collaborationist party; to defile the Temple was to infringe the rights and laws of the priests; and the Romans, Tertullus hoped, would take the side of the pro-Roman party.[6]

Think of the fear and anger Paul must have felt as he listened to these cruel lies. He'd done nothing wrong; yet in this intimidating courtroom, standing before this crooked judge, his life was on the line because of their deceit. After Jerusalem, he had hoped that

6. Barclay, *The Acts of the Apostles*, p. 169.

things would get better, but now they were worse. From the frying pan, he had jumped into the fire.

Some Practical Lessons

At the right moment, Paul will launch a verbal defense. But for now he handles the pressure by remaining silent. From this response, we can extrapolate two principles concerning what to do when things go from bad to worse.

First, *refuse to wrestle; start to rest.* When we wrestle, we panic, don't think clearly, and speak in haste. We try to find ways to pin our accuser to the mat, we concentrate on our strategy and rights. But when things are getting out of hand, it is a time for self-control and silence—a time to rest in God's faithfulness and to wrap up our burdens in a bundle and leave them with Him.

Second, *release the pressure; claim God's peace.* An ancient saying speaks to us in our modern, pressure-filled lives: "You will soon break the bow if you keep it always stretched."[7] In other words, we must release the pressure in our lives or we'll become irritable, anxious, and eventually broken. The first step toward release is claiming God's peace . . . but that peace is not found in our TV-blaring, traffic-racing lifestyles. It's found in silence.

Today, won't you take at least fifteen minutes for silence? Don't fall asleep! Just be quiet, focus on the Lord, and let all the tension filter away from your spirit. During the rest of the day, you may be jumping back and forth between the frying pan and the fire, but let this be a time of restoration. Let this be a time to gather strength.

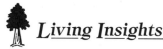 *Living Insights*   STUDY ONE

The problem with trying to be silent is that your thoughts can bounce this way and that like Ping-Pong balls dropped on a tile floor. How do you corral them? Meditation.

When we hear the word *meditation*, we sometimes imagine a person sitting on the floor with his or her legs tied up like a pretzel, thinking about what it would be like to be purple. That is not biblical meditation. But neither is the image of the person laboring

---

7. Phaedrus, as quoted in *The Home Book of Quotations*, 10th ed., comp. Burton Stevenson (New York, N.Y.: Dodd, Mead, and Co., 1967), p. 1100.

behind a deskful of ten-pound books, studying the nuances of the word *Maher-shalal-hash-baz*.

In his book *Spiritual Disciplines for the Christian Life*, Donald S. Whitney provides us with a definition of meditation:

> Let's define meditation as deep thinking on the truths and spiritual realities revealed in Scripture for the purposes of understanding, application, and prayer. Meditation goes beyond hearing, reading, studying, and even memorizing as a means of taking in God's Word. A simple analogy would be a cup of tea. You are the cup of hot water and the intake of Scripture is represented by the tea bag. Hearing God's Word is like one dip of the tea bag into the cup. Some of the tea's flavor is absorbed by the water, but not as much as would occur with a more thorough soaking of the bag. In this analogy, reading, studying, and memorizing God's Word are represented by additional plunges of the tea bag into the cup. . . . Meditation, however, is like immersing the bag completely and letting it steep until all the rich tea flavor has been extracted and the hot water is thoroughly tinctured reddish brown.[8]

Ready to make some meditation tea? In the next Living Insight, we'll show you how.

🌲 *Living Insights*   STUDY TWO

Let's begin learning how to meditate by reading the first two verses of Psalm 1.

> How blessed is the man who does not walk in the
>   counsel of the wicked,
> Nor stand in the path of sinners,
> Nor sit in the seat of scoffers!
> But his delight is in the law of the Lord,
> And in His law he meditates day and night.

---

8. Donald S. Whitney, *Spiritual Disciplines for the Christian Life* (Colorado Springs, Colo.: NavPress, 1991), p. 44.

Now follow these steps, adapted from Donald Whitney, as you meditate.[9]

1. Repeat the verses emphasizing different words. For instance, read the first phrase, "How *blessed* is the man who does *not* walk in the counsel of the wicked." Think about what *blessed* means and how it relates to refraining from wickedness. Then read the phrase, "How blessed is the man who does not *walk* in the *counsel* of the wicked." Meditate on the ways a person can walk in someone else's counsel. As you progress, different lights will turn on in your mind about the implications of the text.

2. Rewrite the verses in your own words. Think of synonyms for the words you take for granted. Also try putting the verses in the first person: "How happy I am when I don't follow worldly advice. . . ."

3. Ask questions that help you apply the verses. Is God teaching you something about Himself? Something to praise or trust Him for? Something to pray about? Some new attitude to adopt? Some decision to make? Some action to take? Some sin to forsake?

4. Finally, pray as you meditate. As the Puritan writer William Bridge advised,

> Begin with reading or hearing. Go on with meditation; end in prayer. . . . [for] reading without meditation is unfruitful; meditation without reading is hurtful; to meditate and to read without prayer upon both, is without blessing.[10]

You've already started with Psalm 1. Why don't you continue reading, meditating, and praying your way through the rest of the Psalms, a little every day? Remember, it is better to digest only a few verses, even a few phrases, at a time than to race through a chapter per day without meditation. Take your time, and savor God's Word.

---

9. Adapted from Whitney, *Spiritual Disciplines*, pp. 49, 55, 50.

10. William Bridge, as quoted by Whitney in *Spiritual Disciplines*, p. 69.

Chapter 13

MAN'S FAVORITE EXCUSE

Acts 24:10–27

Once below a time, Satan called together his evil spirits and growled, "We are losing too many humans to the other side! How can we hold on to the ones we have before they (shudder) slip away to the Enemy?"

One spirit slinked forward. "Master, let's tell them there is no God."

Satan snarled, "Not good enough, imbecile! All creation cries out His existence." The thought of that concept caused him to writhe on his throne and lash those near him with his fiery whips.

A second spirit rose up. "Great One, let's tell them there is no hell."

"Is that the best you can do?" Satan roared, and he shrieked curses so evil that the assembly cowered and trembled.

Finishing his tirade, Satan slumped back, smoldering. Out of the shadows a final dark spirit glided up to him. "Eminence, we have been looking at this problem all wrong. Let them believe that there is a God, even that there is a Savior, and that there is a hell. But let us whisper in their ears, 'There is no hurry.'"

For a moment, Satan sat motionless. Then, slowly, he grinned and finally let out a hideous laugh that echoed through hell for a thousand thousand years.[1]

A fanciful story, yes—but one with a pointed message: Satan doesn't have to convince us to reject the truth, just to put it off. That ruse was most effective on Governor Felix when, confronted with the gospel during Paul's defense of himself, he used mankind and Satan's favorite excuse: "Tomorrow I'll believe, but for today there is no hurry."

Review of the Accusations

Tertullus has just finished charging that Paul is a revolutionary, a leader of a fanatic cult, and has tried to desecrate the temple (see Acts 24:2–6). All the while, Paul has remained silent, quietly trusting God. When the hired orator finally rolls his last *r* and parades

---

1. Adapted from *Biblical Treasury*, as quoted by Paul Lee Tan, *Encyclopedia of 7,700 Illustrations: Signs of the Times* (Chicago, Ill.: Assurance Publishers, 1979), p. 1223.

his last accusation, Felix turns to Paul and gives him a simple nod (v. 10a). Now it's Paul's turn.

Answers to Each Charge

Paul begins by addressing Felix, not with Tertullus' dripping flattery, but with polite honesty.

> "Knowing that for many years you have been a judge to this nation, I cheerfully make my defense." (v. 10b)

By using the word *cheerfully*, Paul communicates a positive attitude despite the treatment he's recently received. Neither vindictive nor irritated, he's confident and yields to Christ control of his emotions. In that frame of mind, he counters Tertullus' first charge.

"I Am Innocent of Being a Troublemaker"

Paul immediately seeks to prove he is not a revolutionary by calling attention to a few key facts.

> "You can take note of the fact that no more than twelve days ago I went up to Jerusalem to worship. And neither in the temple, nor in the synagogues, nor in the city itself did they find me carrying on a discussion with anyone or causing a riot. Nor can they prove to you the charges of which they now accuse me." (vv. 11–13)

By rephrasing Paul's words, Ray Stedman skillfully reveals Paul's three arguments.

> "First, I have had no time to incite a riot. It is only twelve days since I went up to Jerusalem, and I've been absent from the province for years before that. You can't get a riot going in twelve days. Second, I made absolutely no effort to do so. I've never even been seen disputing with anybody, either in the temple or in the synagogues or in the city. . . . And third, no proof whatsoever has been offered for any of the claims made against me."[2]

2. Ray Stedman, *Acts 21–28: Triumphs of the Body* (Santa Ana, Calif.: Vision House Publishers, 1981), p. 68.

Upon making that final point, Paul could rest his case and win the day. But he wants to address Tertullus' second charge, for it broaches Paul's favorite subject—Christianity.

"I Am Innocent of Leading a Cult"

Not willing to let the label *sect*, which is Tertullus' euphemism for *cult*, slip by, Paul next establishes the legitimacy of Christianity as a religion.

> "This I admit to you, that according to the Way which they call a sect I do serve the God of our fathers, believing everything that is in accordance with the Law, and that is written in the Prophets; having a hope in God, which these men cherish themselves, that there shall certainly be a resurrection of both the righteous and the wicked. In view of this, I also do my best to maintain always a blameless conscience both before God and before men." (vv. 14–16)

In these verses, Paul presents four pieces of evidence about his faith that make it acceptable. First, he serves the same God the Jews do; second, he believes the same Word of God; third, he, too, hopes in God for his future resurrection; and fourth, concerning his beliefs and lifestyle, he has a completely clear conscience.

Making a particular impact on the governor was probably Paul's last statement about having a blameless conscience. How Felix must have longed to discover relief from the sins of deceit, treachery, and betrayal that diseased his political life. And that same longing applied to his personal life as well, for it was nearly gangrenous with sin. F. F. Bruce explains that Felix's present wife, Drusilla, was his third, and

> when she was still only sixteen, Felix, with the help of a Cypriote magician called Atomos, persuaded her to leave her husband and marry him.[3]

Spiritually and emotionally, Felix was ailing, and suddenly here comes Paul exuding inner health. So the governor, his interest

3. F. F. Bruce, *Commentary on the Book of the Acts*, The New International Commentary on the New Testament (Grand Rapids, Mich.: William B. Eerdmans Publishing Co., 1954), pp. 472–73.

piqued, listens intently to Paul's arguments—the next of which refers to Tertullus' charge that Paul defiled the temple.

"I Am Innocent of Desecrating the Temple"

Paul asserts that he had not gone to the temple to tear it down, but to support it.

> "Now after several years I came to bring alms to my nation and to present offerings; in which they found me occupied in the temple, having been purified, without any crowd or uproar. But there were certain Jews from Asia . . ." (vv. 17–18)

It was the Jews from Asia, you'll recall, who initiated the uproar. And it is they, Paul continues,

> "who ought to have been present before you, and to make accusation, if they should have anything against me. Or else let these men themselves tell what misdeed they found when I stood before the Council, other than for this one statement which I shouted out while standing among them, 'For the resurrection of the dead I am on trial before you today.'" (vv. 19–21)

Paul closes his case with the issue of the resurrection of the dead. In so doing, he makes it clear that this is a religious, not civil, matter and that he should be freed.

Felix, however, is caught in a sticky dilemma. He knows Paul is innocent, yet he must also appease the powerful Jews before him. So he procrastinates, saying, "When Lysias the commander comes down, I will decide your case" (v. 22b). Then, to calm his conscience for unnecessarily delaying Paul's release, he gives him a light sentence and extends him freedom to see his friends (v. 23b).

Through his actions, we see Felix avoiding a difficult political decision. We also see evidence of spiritual dallying when Luke states, "Felix, *having a more exact knowledge about the Way*, put them off" (v. 22a, emphasis added). Even before Paul spoke, Felix apparently knew some facts about Christ—at least enough facts to be saved.[4]

---

4. Felix could have come in contact with Christianity through his Jewish wife or through Philip the evangelist and the disciples who lived in Caesarea (see Acts 21:8, 16).

But he was still unwilling to repent and trust Christ. "There is no hurry," Felix was saying. "There is plenty of time to come to Jesus."

Subsequent Hearings: Private Audience

Demonstrating divine patience, the Lord gives Felix another opportunity to hear Paul explain the gospel.

Felix and Drusilla

Some days later, Felix arrived with Drusilla, his wife who was a Jewess, and sent for Paul, and heard him speak about faith in Christ Jesus. (v. 24)

Concerning this verse, one commentator points out:

The Western text indicates that Drusilla persuaded Felix to let her listen to Paul: "Felix came with his wife Drusilla, who was a Jewess, *who asked to see Paul and hear the word. Wishing therefore to satisfy her,* he summoned Paul."[5]

If that ancient Greek source is correct, Drusilla's background may provide us with an explanation of why she especially wanted to hear Paul. A young woman, she was already in her second marriage, having been seduced away from her first husband by the more experienced Felix. In addition, she had been raised in a family rife with wickedness and turmoil.[6] Perhaps in Paul's Jesus she saw hope for a clean conscience and a chance for a new beginning.

So the Apostle speaks to her and Felix not about marriage and family themes, but about "faith in Christ Jesus" and "righteousness, self-control and the judgment to come" (vv. 24b, 25a). They had to settle these issues first of all. However, instead of repenting and trusting,

Felix became frightened and said, "Go away for the present, and when I find time, I will summon you." (v. 25b)

---

5. Simon J. Kistemaker, *New Testament Commentary: Exposition of the Acts of the Apostles* (Grand Rapids, Mich.: Baker Book House, 1990), p. 851.

6. Her father, Herod Agrippa I, had executed Jesus' disciple James and was later struck down by God when the people honored him as divine (Acts 12:1–2; 20–23). Her aunt and great uncle, Herodias and Herod Antipas, had John the Baptist beheaded (Mark 6:16–29). Her grandfather, Herod Aristobulus, was strangled by order of his own father, Herod the Great— the king at the time of Jesus' birth who ordered the killing of all the Bethlehem baby boys (Matt. 2:1–18).

In spite of Drusilla's nudgings and his own conscience stirring him with divine fear, Felix once again put off responding to Christ. Paul had held a cup of truth before his spiritually parched lips, yet he still refused to drink it. He knew there was a Savior, a heaven, and a hell, but tragically, he decided that there was no hurry to do anything about it.

Felix Alone

Over the next two years, Felix did see Paul again several times, but his conscience turned to steel as procrastination and greed hardened his heart (v. 27a). Remembering Paul's mention of the alms he brought to the temple (v. 17), Felix quickly reverted to his corrupt ways, for

> he was hoping that money would be given him by Paul; therefore he also used to send for him quite often and converse with him. (v. 26)

Finally, as often occurred in Roman politics, he fell from power and

> was succeeded by Porcius Festus; and wishing to do the Jews a favor, Felix left Paul imprisoned.[7] (v. 27b)

Scripture does not tell us what happened to Felix and his troubled wife Drusilla. We hope they later trusted Christ, but Satan's sly "no-hurry" tactic may have delayed them until it was too late.

Response Today

This brief but telling episode in Felix's life exposes two warnings about putting off God's truth. First, *delay dulls the edge of the sword of the Spirit.* Each time we say, "Tomorrow, Lord," the Spirit's pricking and prodding becomes less effective. Eventually, we give little more than a lethargic yawn in response to God's truth. When that happens, a procrastinatory callous has formed over our hearts, and although the Spirit stabs us with conviction, we may not feel a thing.

Second, *delay blinds the mind with lesser issues.* For Felix, as soon as he had conveniently shifted the spiritual issue to the back burner, another less important matter came forward—money. In your life,

---

7. Felix lost his governorship because he violently put down a riot in Caesarea, murdering many Jewish leaders. See Bruce, *Acts*, p. 474. Perhaps he thought that by leaving Paul in prison he could regain the Jews' favor and therefore his superiors'.

have you pushed aside a spiritual concern and let other things fill your view? Take hold of that Spirit-prompted issue, and take action right away. For there is a Savior, there is forgiveness, and there is hope for a new beginning. But there is no guarantee of tomorrow, so hurry!

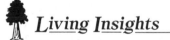

Living Insights

. Do you struggle with procrastination? Has keeping up with this study on Acts been difficult for you? Things like Bible study, prayer, or getting involved in accountability groups can be a real trial for some Christians, since they constantly have to overcome the obstacle of their own inertia.

What issue in your life has prompted you to put the Spirit on hold? He's waiting patiently on the line to talk to you. You see the red light flashing, but perhaps you've been afraid to pick up the receiver and push the button.

Right now, in a quiet moment, admit your fear to Him; then go ahead and release the hold button. After you've listened to Him for awhile, write down what it is that He wants to change in your life—an attitude He wants you to cultivate, a habit to develop, or a sin to forsake.

_____

_____

_____

What are some steps you can take today to begin fulfilling His desire for your life?

_____

_____

_____

_____

Share these steps with someone close to you, so that he or she can hold you accountable. And continue to keep the lines open between you and the Lord; He may call again at any time.

Living Insights

Imagine that inside your conscience is a large, sharp-edged box. And that each time you sin, the box turns, causing a corner to prick your conscience. Commit that same sin again, and the corner nicks you again. However, as that sin becomes a habit, the corners are worn down little by little, resulting in less and less pain in your conscience. Eventually, sin smooths the box into a harmless ball. When you sin, you feel nothing.

Has a certain sin in your life been eroding the sensitivity of your conscience? If so, what is that sin?

_____

_____

God has given us confession as a tool to restore the effectiveness of our consciences. Psalm 51 is David's prayer of confession after committing adultery with Bathsheba and making sure that her husband was killed in battle (2 Sam. 11). Read the psalm for an example, and then write out your own confession.

_____

_____

_____

_____

James also instructed us to confess our sins to another (James 5:16a). Reveal your struggle with sin to someone you can trust, someone who'll pray with you, and you'll sense your conscience being quickly revitalized. Soon, when tempted, you'll wince at that inner pricking once again.

Chapter 14

DISCIPLINES THAT CULTIVATE MATURITY

Acts 25:1–22

*D*iscipline. It's not one of our favorite words, is it? With this term comes images of punishment—standing in the corner, getting sent to your room, being grounded. We chafe at the thought of it, not only because receiving it is distasteful, but because it so noticeably brings to the fore our own failure and wrongdoing.

Jesus, however, would have us broaden our image of discipline. More than punishment and correction, much divine discipline is rooted in a deep care for our ongoing growth and maturity. Listen as Jesus explains this.

> "I am the true vine, and My Father is the vinedresser. Every branch in Me that does not bear fruit, He takes away; and *every branch that bears fruit, He prunes it, that it may bear more fruit.*" (John 15:1–2, emphasis added)

In this next episode of Paul's life, we'll see God painstakingly pruning His fruitful apostle. Not because Paul's done anything wrong, and not because God is capricious or cruel, but because "by this is My Father glorified, that you bear much fruit" (v. 8a).

Scriptures in Support of Discipline

Before we take a look at Paul's process of pruning, let's peek into Proverbs for a better understanding of the Vinedresser's perspective of discipline.

> My son, do not reject the discipline of the Lord,[1]
> Or loathe His reproof,[2]
> For whom the Lord loves He reproves,
> Even as a father, the son in whom he delights.
> (Prov. 3:11–12)

1. The Hebrew word for *reject* is *maas*, which means "to refuse or despise" and is related to an Arabic word that means "to lightly esteem."

2. The Hebrew word for *loathe* is *quts*, which means "abhorrence or sickening dread."

Notice that the Lord commands us to welcome discipline when it comes knocking, for it carries in its hand a lesson from our loving Father.[3] Expanding this concept, the writer to the Hebrews explains further features of God's discipline:

> It is for discipline that you endure; God deals with you as with sons; for what son is there whom his father does not discipline? But if you are without discipline, of which all have become partakers, then you are illegitimate children and not sons. Furthermore, we had earthly fathers to discipline us, and we respected them; shall we not much rather be subject to the Father of spirits, and live? For they disciplined us for a short time as seemed best to them, but He disciplines us for our good, that we may share His holiness. All discipline for the moment seems not to be joyful, but sorrowful; yet to those who have been trained by it, afterwards it yields the peaceful fruit of righteousness. (Heb. 12:7–11)

These verses paint the glowing positives of God's discipline: it verifies that we belong to Him, giving us security; it has a purpose— our good; and although it is initially uncomfortable, its benefit of holiness outweighs the pain.

Now, with these thoughts on discipline as a backdrop, we come to the apostle Paul and the disciplines that entered his life— hardships that God used, not to punish him, but to prune him into an even more fruitful witness for Christ.

Paul's Growth through God's Disciplines

If discipline assures us of God's love, then Paul must have felt adored! In this episode, his life was trimmed back with not one but four tools, and all of the cutting away took place in the painful context of prison. Let's look now at the first tool God used.

Prolonged Delay

Even though he knew Paul was innocent, Governor Felix would not release him. So for two long years the Apostle twiddled his

---

3. For the kinds of lessons God teaches us through discipline, see Romans 5:3–5 and James 1:2–4.

thumbs in jail, conversing with Felix from time to time, but mostly just waiting.

For Paul, this delay must have been frustrating. He was a man driven by a passion to make disciples of all nations. In keeping with that passion, God had promised to send him to Rome (Acts 23:11), but here he sat in Caesarea . . . in prison.

His hopes for release must have been heightened when he heard that Festus was going to replace Felix as governor. Surely Felix would obey his conscience and dismiss him before leaving! But crushingly, "wishing to do the Jews a favor, Felix left Paul imprisoned" (24:27b). And when Festus took office, he continued to keep Paul in custody (see 25:4, 21).

In the past, Paul had been God's chief traveling witness, but now he was stuck in a mire of Roman bureaucracy. As the days dragged on, Paul's thoughts must have spun wildly: *Lord, how can I preach to the world if I can't get out of Caesarea? Have You set me aside for a reason? Are You through using me?*

Actually, God was planning to use Paul in even greater ways, but He had to teach him lessons about patience, endurance, and humility—reproofs that he could learn only through the discipline of delay.

False Accusations

Not long after Festus becomes the new governor, he travels to Jerusalem to meet with the religious leaders there. Immediately,

> the chief priests and the leading men of the Jews brought charges against Paul; and they were urging him, requesting a concession against Paul, that he might have him brought to Jerusalem (at the same time, setting an ambush to kill him on the way). (25:2–3)

Two years have passed since Paul's escape and his defense before Felix, yet these Jews are still bitterly determined to see him dead. Festus, unaware of their vicious designs, invites them to Caesarea to once again present their charges against Paul (vv. 4–5). The Jews eagerly step through this open door, hoping Festus will agree to order Paul back to Jerusalem and into their trap.

Back in Caesarea, Festus clears the docket and summons a surprised Paul to stand trial again (v. 6).

And after he had arrived, the Jews who had come down from Jerusalem stood around him, bringing many and serious charges against him which they could not prove. (v. 7)

Stalked and surrounded by his ravenous enemies, Paul nevertheless stays strong:

"I have committed no offense either against the Law of the Jews or against the temple or against Caesar." (v. 8)

Unfair Exploitation

As Paul makes his uncompromising defense, he can probably tell by the look on Festus' face that his chances for release are vanishing. The new governor is already toying with a way to use Paul for his own advantage.

Festus, wishing to do the Jews a favor, answered Paul and said, "Are you willing to go up to Jerusalem and stand trial before me on these charges?" (v. 9)

Just like the unscrupulous Felix, Festus was playing a political game—with Paul as his trump card. "You want Paul? I'll give you Paul," he was telling the Jews, "but you'll owe me one." Festus didn't care about the facts of the case or about Paul as a person; he was only interested in furthering his career.

As a result, Paul felt the sharp edge of the pruning shears come near him again—the discipline of unfair exploitation. But through this experience, Paul developed courage, as evidenced by his response to Festus:

"I am standing before Caesar's tribunal, where I ought to be tried. I have done no wrong to the Jews, as you also very well know. If then I am a wrongdoer, and have committed anything worthy of death, I do not refuse to die; but if none of those things is true of which these men accuse me, no one can hand me over to them. I appeal to Caesar." (vv. 10b–12)

As a Roman citizen, Paul had the right to ask that Caesar decide his case. So, bravely confronting the governor and confounding the Jews, Paul lays down *his* trump card, which forces Festus to rethink his plan.

Then when Festus had conferred with his council, he answered, "You have appealed to Caesar, to Caesar you shall go." (v. 12)

With those words and the pound of the gavel, Paul's trial before Festus is over. However, he remains in custody, unsure about the implications of his appeal to Caesar or what will happen next.

Continued Uncertainty

Several days later, King Agrippa and his sister Bernice come to Caesarea to greet the new governor (v. 13).[4] In the course of their conversations, Festus comes around to the subject of Paul and recounts the events that led up to the trial (vv. 14–17). His summary of the issues involved, however, reveals how ill-equipped he is to judge Paul's case. He tells Agrippa,

> "They simply had some points of disagreement with
> him about their own religion and about a certain
> dead man, Jesus, whom Paul asserted to be alive.
> And being at a loss how to investigate such matters,
> I asked whether he was willing to go to Jerusalem
> and there stand trial on these matters. But when
> Paul appealed to be held in custody for the Emperor's
> decision, I ordered him to be kept in custody until
> I send him to Caesar." And Agrippa said to Festus,
> "I also would like to hear the man myself." "Tomor-
> row," he said, "you shall hear him." (vv. 19–22)

Isn't it interesting how Festus refers to Jesus—"a certain dead man . . . whom Paul asserted to be alive"? He was completely ignorant of Christianity and the person of Jesus Christ, yet he had a hand in deciding Paul's fate. How could he decide Paul's case wisely? And what kind of justice could Paul expect from the morally corrupt Agrippa and Bernice?

Imagine the uncertainty of his predicament. He had no control over the accuracy of the information being given about him, and he had no say in any of the decisions made about him. Instead, like

---

4. King Agrippa is Herod Agrippa II, the Jewish ruler of a small territory northeast of Palestine. He had two sisters, Drusilla and Bernice. The latter sister had been married to Agrippa's predecessor and uncle, King Herod of Chalcis. Upon her husband's death, Bernice lived with Herod Agrippa II in what was rumored to be an incestuous relationship.

some court jester, he would be called upon to perform at the whim and convenience of his captors.

How easy it is at times like these to doubt our value and worth in God's eyes. Yet throughout this discipline of uncertainty, Paul held fast to his faith, as we will see in the next chapter, through his witness for his steadfast and dependable Lord.

How All This Relates to Us

Most of us can identify with Paul's pain during this ordeal, because we've each endured times of lengthy delay, false accusations, unfair exploitation, or continued uncertainty. He made it through, though, and we can too. We just need to remember that these hardships are part of God's pruning process—a process that includes three encouraging facts: It proves our Father cares. It removes any impurities from our lives. And the benefit will be a mature character of strength, life, and beauty.

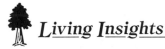 *Living Insights* STUDY ONE

Can you identify with the hardships Paul endured in Caesarea? Which of them comes most readily to mind?

❑ prolonged delay   ❑ unfair exploitation

❑ false accusation   ❑ continued uncertainty

Take a moment to describe the situation, your feelings, and your response.

_____

_____

_____

_____

One key to handling these pruning circumstances is having a correct view of God. Some people see the "Father in Heaven as a grandfather in heaven," wrote C. S. Lewis—

a senile benevolence who, as they say, "liked to see young people enjoying themselves," and whose plan for the universe was simply that it might be truly said at the end of each day, "a good time was had by all."[5]

Discipline and hard times are jarring to people who hold that view of God. They feel cheated and angry because they aren't getting the happiness they think God owes them.

Others may swing to the opposite extreme and view God as a scowling schoolmarm ready to rap their knuckles if they swerve an inch from the straight and narrow. To them, difficulties in life are expected and endured with bitter toleration.

During your pruning process, have you viewed God from either of these perspectives? If not, in what other way have you been picturing God? How has your attitude toward God affected your attitude toward your situation?

_____

_____

_____

_____

In the next Living Insight, we'll examine another way to picture God that will help you endure your painful experience. But for now, take a moment to admit to the Lord any attitudes of anger, bitterness, or blame in your heart. Reveal to Him your doubts and frustrations. Being honest about your feelings toward Him is a solid first step toward coping with your pain.

Living Insights   STUDY TWO

How does God want us to view Him during our days of discipline? The Lord gave Jeremiah a snapshot of Himself when He commanded him, "Arise and go down to the potter's house." Read the account in Jeremiah 18:1–6 as well as Isaiah's words in Isaiah 64:8.

As a potter, God has a mental image of what He wants us to become—a graceful, strong, intricately designed vessel into which

---

5. C. S. Lewis, *The Problem of Pain* (New York, N.Y.: Macmillan Publishing Co., 1962), p. 40.

He can pour Himself in overflowing measure. So in His passion, He presses and works us, spins and molds us, not because He wants to hurt us, but because He wants to honor us.

"It is natural," C. S. Lewis observes,

> for us to wish that God had designed for us a less glorious and less arduous destiny; but then we are wishing not for more love but for less.[6]

How can viewing God as an artist and yourself as His work in progress transform your attitude?

_____

_____

_____

What are the practical ramifications in your life of such an attitude?

_____

_____

_____

Pruning *is* painful; that fact cannot be denied. But in many ways, some of which we will never understand, it brings about good in us. As Philip Yancey has expressed it: "Suffering *produces* something. It has value; it changes us."[7]

Won't you begin yielding to God's pruning today?

6. Lewis, The Problem of Pain, p. 43.

7. Philip Yancey, Where Is God When It Hurts?, rev. and exp. (Grand Rapids, Mich.: Zondervan Publishing House, 1990), p. 108.

Chapter 15

ALMOST PERSUADED . . . BUT NOT QUITE

Acts 25:23–26:32

Think of the emotion packed into the word *almost*. For example: it's five seconds to the buzzer, the home team is down by one point, and the crowd's favorite player has the basketball. Quickly he moves into position. He jumps! He shoots! The ball arches up to the hoop, bounces twice on the rim . . . and falls away. As the buzzer sounds, the fans let out a collective moan—their team almost won the game.

Almost won—the two words together are gut-wrenching. There's no second chance; there's no trophy for the most "almost wins"; there are no cheers, no banners, no victory dances. It doesn't matter how close the team came to winning; the game is over, and they lost.

Spiritually speaking, the words *almost saved* are just as final but have far more sobering consequences. As C. H. Spurgeon wrote:

> Almost persuaded to be a Christian is like the man who was almost pardoned, but he was hanged; like the man who was almost rescued, but he was burned in the house. A man that is almost saved is damned.[1]

In the following passage, Paul carefully aims the gospel message toward King Agrippa, hoping to win him to Christ. The truth arches through the king's mind, bounces twice on the rim of his heart . . . will it fall away?

Setting the Stage

Paul's speech before Agrippa will be his sixth and final defense of Christianity recorded in Acts.[2] The setting is a large courtroom called simply "the auditorium" (25:23). However, the room was anything but simple. Heavy tapestries probably adorned the walls,

---

1. C. H. Spurgeon, *Spurgeon at His Best*, comp. Tom Carter (Grand Rapids, Mich.: Baker Book House, 1988), p. 315.

2. For information on all six speeches, see the chart "Survey of Six Defenses of the Faith" on page 90.

125

with marble pillars vaulting upward to meet the ornately carved ceiling. At the far end of the room gleamed the rich, polished wood of the judges' benches and the golden royal thrones with their crimson cushions.

As the doors open with slow majesty, King Agrippa and Bernice flow into the room in their purple robes

> amid great pomp . . . accompanied by the com-
> manders and the prominent men of the city. (v. 23a)

The word *pomp* in Greek is *phantasia*, meaning "show, display."[3] The entourage must have entered the room with a showy parade of elegance and power. Then, in stark contrast, Luke writes, "at the command of Festus, Paul was brought in" (v. 23b). What irony! Paul, an heir to the very kingdom of heaven, with the freedom of the Son of God granted to him, must stand before this pretentious, immoral court in chains!

With the prisoner now present, the trial begins. Festus opens the case by explaining his purpose for arranging this hearing.

> "King Agrippa, and all you gentlemen here present with us, you behold this man about whom all the people of the Jews appealed to me, both at Jerusalem and here, loudly declaring that he ought not to live any longer. But I found that he had committed noth-ing worthy of death; and since he himself appealed to the Emperor, I decided to send him. Yet I have nothing definite about him to write to my lord. Therefore I have brought him before you all and especially before you, King Agrippa, so that after the investigation has taken place, I may have something to write. For it seems absurd to me in sending a prisoner, not to indicate also the charges against him." (vv. 24–27)

In custody for over two years and having already endured five trials, Paul had still not been charged with any crime! And soon he would be going to Rome to stand trial before Caesar, yet accord-ing to Festus, he'd done nothing wrong. So what could the new

---

3. G. Abbott-Smith, *A Manual Greek Lexicon of the New Testament*, 3d ed. (Edinburgh, Scotland: T. and T. Clark, 1937), p. 466.

governor write to the Emperor? "Here's Paul. He's on trial for . . . nothing in particular."

Festus hoped that Agrippa would be able to sort out the religious issues and help him write something reasonable to Nero. The Jewish leader sought to oblige him, and Festus gladly gave him control of the hearing.

> And Agrippa said to Paul, "You are permitted to speak for yourself." Then Paul stretched out his hand and proceeded to make his defense. (26:1)

Declaring the Defense

In what may be his finest hour, Paul gets to tell of Christ's purpose and power to influential King Agrippa. For despite his showy protocol and intimidating power, this ruler lives in chains—the chains of sin. In order to bring him to freedom, Paul—as we've seen him do so many times before—first begins to build a bridge that Agrippa can cross securely.

> "In regard to all the things of which I am accused by the Jews, I consider myself fortunate, King Agrippa, that I am about to make my defense before you today; especially because you are an expert in all customs and questions among the Jews; therefore I beg you to listen to me patiently." (vv. 2–3)

From this launching point of Jewish customs, Paul will build his bridge in three sections, each bringing Agrippa and the others present closer to a new, divine realm of everlasting mercy and joy. The first span Paul extends is his own devoutly Jewish life before he met Christ.

Before Christ

> "So then, all Jews know my manner of life from my youth up, which from the beginning was spent among my own nation and at Jerusalem; since they have known about me for a long time previously, if they are willing to testify, that I lived as a Pharisee according to the strictest sect of our religion. And now I am standing trial for the hope of the promise made by God to our fathers; the promise to which our twelve tribes hope to attain, as they earnestly

serve God night and day. And for this hope, O King, I am being accused by Jews. Why is it considered incredible among you people if God does raise the dead?" (vv. 4–8)

Stopping construction for a moment, Paul turns from Agrippa and searches the others' souls with his pointed question about resurrection. *Don't just sit there listening to an interesting story,* he seems to say; *think about your own beliefs, your own hopes. Is God's power real to you or not?* Then, having secured everyone's attention, he resumes his focus on Agrippa.

> "So then, I thought to myself that I had to do many things hostile to the name of Jesus of Nazareth. And this is just what I did in Jerusalem; not only did I lock up many of the saints in prisons, having received authority from the chief priests, but also when they were being put to death I cast my vote against them. And as I punished them often in all the synagogues, I tried to force them to blaspheme; and being furiously enraged at them, I kept pursuing them even to foreign cities." (vv. 9–11)

Why does Paul make so much of his days as a persecutor of the church? To establish his credibility with Agrippa, who, like his sister Drusilla, comes from a long line of Christian-haters. Agrippa's great-grandfather Herod the Great conducted the search-and-destroy mission against the infant Jesus, his great-uncle Herod Antipas murdered John the Baptist, and his father, Herod Agrippa I, executed James and imprisoned Peter. Agrippa "knew" how committed Jews were to treat threatening Christians. Paul says to him, "I used to be just like that."

And Agrippa, who was probably expecting some wild-eyed, Scripture-spouting loon, is faced with a man who isn't so different from himself; a man whose realness is transparent and surprisingly believable. With this crucial link firmly established, Paul moves forward to the day his life turned toward a strange, new course.

Conversion Experience

Paul continues with a telling phrase: "While thus engaged" (v. 12a). He had been on no spiritual quest, gnawed by doubts about his course. He had still been single-mindedly engaged in pursuing

128

his vendetta against Christians when Christ stopped him on the Damascus road. And in his simple, straightforward manner, he tells of this life-changing encounter.

> "At midday, O King, I saw on the way a light from heaven, brighter than the sun, shining all around me and those who were journeying with me. And when we had all fallen to the ground, I heard a voice saying to me in the Hebrew dialect, 'Saul, Saul, why are you persecuting Me? It is hard for you to kick against the goads.' And I said, 'Who art Thou, Lord?' And the Lord said, 'I am Jesus whom you are persecuting. But arise, and stand on your feet; for this purpose I have appeared to you, to appoint you a minister and a witness not only to the things which you have seen, but also to the things in which I will appear to you; delivering you from the Jewish people and from the Gentiles, to whom I am sending you.'"
> (vv. 13–17)

With three down-to-earth phrases—"I saw . . . I heard . . . I said"—Paul takes Agrippa from the pride of Pharisees to the majesty of Christ. Then, just as authentically, he explains Christ's plan for him and the world.

> "'To open their eyes so that they may turn from darkness to light and from the dominion of Satan to God, in order that they may receive forgiveness of sins and an inheritance among those who have been sanctified by faith in Me.'" (v. 18)

What a concise, believable, and coherent statement of Christianity! Paul does not smother the truth with a syrupy appeal, terrify Agrippa with God's wrath and the torments of hell, or alter the gospel to make it more palatable. Addressing the king person to person, sinner to sinner, he gives him the simple facts. The simple facts of Christ's mercy, generosity, and love.

After Salvation

But just knowing the facts isn't enough. Agrippa must respond in faith, so Paul describes what that faith has looked like in his own life.

"Consequently, King Agrippa, I did not prove disobedient to the heavenly vision, but kept declaring both to those of Damascus first, and also at Jerusalem and then throughout all the region of Judea, and even to the Gentiles, that they should repent and turn to God, performing deeds appropriate to repentance. For this reason some Jews seized me in the temple and tried to put me to death. And so, having obtained help from God, I stand to this day testifying both to small and great, stating nothing but what the Prophets and Moses said was going to take place; that the Christ was to suffer, and that by reason of His resurrection from the dead He should be the first to proclaim light both to the Jewish people and to the Gentiles." (vv. 19–23)

Paul was saying, "I didn't ignore the light and the voice; I obeyed. King Agrippa, you also need to trust Christ and live for Him." But in saying this, Paul wasn't intending to call attention to himself and his faith, but to God and His power. "God has changed my life," Paul was announcing. "And He can change your life too."

Notice that not once did he shake a bony finger of judgment at Agrippa, despite the king's rumored incestuous relationship with his sister Bernice. Instead, he unveiled Christ—the Messiah foretold by the Prophets and Moses, the suffering Jesus nailed to the cross, the shining Savior risen from the dead.

Facing the Facts

Agrippa sat quietly, just listening. Festus, however, had heard enough.

> And while Paul was saying this in his defense, Festus said in a loud voice, "Paul, you are out of your mind! Your great learning is driving you mad." (v. 24)

Irritated with Paul and the gospel, the governor calls him a lunatic. Remaining composed and confident, though, Paul keeps the focus on Christ.

> "I am not out of my mind, most excellent Festus, but I utter words of sober truth. For the king knows about these matters, and I speak to him also with

confidence, since I am persuaded that none of these things escape his notice; for this has not been done in a corner. King Agrippa, do you believe the Prophets? I know that you do." And Agrippa replied to Paul, "In a short time you will persuade me to become a Christian." And Paul said, "I would to God, that whether in a short or long time, not only you, but also all who hear me this day, might become such as I am, except for these chains." (vv. 25–29)

"In a short time you will persuade me to become a Christian." The king seems to be so close to salvation![4] Desperately, Paul pleads with him to trust Christ; but sadly, the truth falls away from the rim of his heart. Agrippa almost became a Christian.

The scene concludes with Festus, Agrippa, and Bernice consulting together on the side about Paul's guilt or innocence (v. 30). "This man is not doing anything worthy of death or imprisonment," they say to one another (v. 31). Then, candidly,

Agrippa said to Festus, "This man might have been set free if he had not appealed to Caesar." (v. 32)

Applying the Appeal

Ironically, although Paul remained in chains, his heart was free in Christ. And although Agrippa enjoyed unlimited freedom and power, his heart was chained in darkness. So in the end, the prisoner was the free man, and the king was the slave.

Out of the irony of this story, two principles shine like beacons. First, *hearing about Christ doesn't automatically bring internal change*. The truths of Christ are like the sun's rays: they either nurture growth or, as in Agrippa's case, harden clay hearts. One's openness to Christ and willingness to obey determine the difference.

Second, *responding to Christ doesn't automatically remove external chains*. Spiritually, Paul was freer than anyone around him, but he still wore chains, and he still had difficulties. However, because of

---

4. Commentators vary widely on what Agrippa was saying here, how he said it, and what he meant by it. His statement has been "variously represented as a trivial jest, a bitter sarcasm, a grave irony, a burst of anger, and an expression of sincere conviction." J. A. Alexander, A Commentary on the Acts of the Apostles, vol. 2, as quoted by John Stott in The Spirit, the Church, and the World: The Message of Acts (Downers Grove, Ill.: InterVarsity Press, 1990), p. 376.

his faith in Christ, he could live with the chains. That's Christ's power in action—not the removal of the hardships, but peace in the midst of them.

Living Insights

Perhaps you have a non-Christian friend who, like Agrippa, is open to Christ. From Paul's defense let's formulate some guidelines that can help you clearly communicate the gospel.

First, *start on common ground.* For Paul and Agrippa, Judaism was their point of identification, because they both had extensive knowledge of Jewish customs (Acts 26:3). What is the common ground you have with your friend?

_____

_____

Second, *as your relationship develops, look for ways to weave in the subject of Christ.* If your common interest is parenting, you can talk about how knowing Christ helps you rear your children. That leads to the subject of knowing Christ as Savior. How can your common interest lead you to the subject of Christ?

_____

_____

Third, *be transparent and honest.* Paul detailed his past hatred of Christians because he wanted to tell Agrippa, "I know where you're coming from." Of course, you don't need to expose every secret to your friend, but being real is vital. In what ways can you open up to your friend?

_____

_____

Fourth, *explain the gospel clearly.* Paul presented Christ positively, emphasizing His desire to bring us out of darkness, out of Satan's cruel realm, into forgiveness, and to an inheritance in heaven (v. 18). He also explained that Christ died and rose from the dead as Savior (v. 23). With Paul's model in mind, explain the gospel message in your own words.

_____

_____

_____

_____

Fifth, *emphasize the need for a decision.* Paul appealed to Agrippa to admit the truth of what he was saying and become a Christian (vv. 26–29). When you talk to your friend, do not forget to provide an opportunity to trust Christ. You may say something like, "Is there anything that is hindering you from trusting Christ right now?"

At that point, the decision is in their hands.

Living Insights   STUDY TWO

How could Paul stay calm under the pressure of his trial? He was experiencing the peace that Jesus had promised when He said:

> "Peace I leave with you; My peace I give to you; not as the world gives, do I give to you. Let not your heart be troubled, nor let it be fearful." (John 14:27)

John White illustrates the peace that Jesus gave Paul:

> The heart that has this kind of peace is like a lighthouse in a storm. Winds shriek, waves crash, lightning flickers around it. But inside, the children play while their parents go about their work. They may look out the window to marvel at the powers that rage around them, but they have peace—the peace of knowing that the strength which protects them is stronger than the strength of the storm.[5]

Trusting Christ for salvation doesn't exempt us from going through storms. But during the storm, we can have peace—that's what Christ promised. Where can you let that peace enter into your life today?

---

5. John White, *Greater Than Riches* (Downers Grove, Ill.: InterVarsity Press, 1992), p. 131.

Chapter 16

HOW TO ENJOY A SHIPWRECK

Acts 27

> Day after miserable day, night after terrifying night, they rose and fell in mountainous seas. Thick unbroken clouds prevented any reckoning: the captain had no idea of the ship's position. . . . The main cargo of wheat had become thoroughly waterlogged—the sacks too heavy and sodden to move in a pitching ship, and all the time increasing in weight.
>
> The water level rose, the ship settled lower, until by the eleventh or twelfth day of the storm "all hope of our being saved was abandoned." Foundering was inevitable now—a matter of a few days at most even if the storm abated—and would mean the loss of all hands if they abandoned ship.[1]

Author John Pollock vividly recaptures the panic, confusion, and near-death experience of the first-century passengers who boarded the ship bound for Rome, as described in Acts 27. Caught in a violent storm, they struggled desperately to keep afloat until eventually everyone—soldiers, seamen, and seafarers—gave up all hope of survival . . . everyone except one, the apostle Paul.

To find out why Paul never lost hope or panicked, let's go back and step aboard that ship and sail along with him on his incredible odyssey to Rome.

Preparation for the Voyage

For years the Apostle has dreamed of visiting the saints in Rome, to encourage their faith. Now, at last, the arrangements are being made that will make that dream reality.

---

1. John Pollock, *The Apostle: A Life of Paul* (Wheaton, Ill.: Scripture Press Publications, Victor Books, 1985), p. 280.

And when it was decided that we should sail for
Italy, they proceeded to deliver Paul and some other
prisoners to a centurion of the Augustan cohort
named Julius. (Acts 27:1)

Stowed compactly away in that one verse are several important
details about the voyage—details that John Pollock explains as if
he were a deckhand leading us aboard the ship.

> Festus handed Paul over to a centurion named
> Julius serving with the imperial or Augustan cohort,
> whose officers and men traveled throughout the em-
> pire on escort and courier duties. Julius commanded
> a detail of about a dozen soldiers: Paul was the only
> prisoner of rank, permitted to take two attendants
> who were listed as his personal slaves: Aristarchus
> and Luke the physician. The other prisoners would
> be convicts on their grim way to "make a Roman
> holiday," either as lion fodder at the games or, if
> burly enough, for training as gladiators. These would
> all be chained to timbers below decks, but Paul and
> his attendants could move about freely, though he
> must always wear a loose chain, symbol of his status.[2]

When God promised Paul two years earlier that he would "witness at Rome" (23:11), the Apostle probably had no idea he would
be shipped there in chains courtesy of the Roman justice system.
But the Lord can use any circumstance to fulfill His word.

The Voyage and Storm

Before we sail, let's first look at a few particulars of our itinerary.

Technical Factors

As you can see from the following map, our journey begins in
Caesarea. It's late August, A.D. 59; the winds are light and westerly;
and Julius has secured our passage aboard a coastal vessel that will
take us to a port of call where the centurion feels confident he will
find another ship sailing for Rome. The plan is to reach the imperial
city by the end of October.

2. Pollock, The Apostle, p. 274.

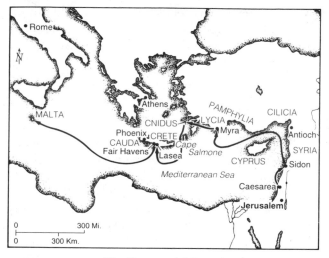

The Trip toward Rome[3]

Keeping record of our journey is the meticulous Dr. Luke. It will be through his eyes that we'll experience this voyage. Let's set sail now from Caesarea.

Physical Dangers

The late summer winds in the eastern Mediterranean prohibit sailing across the open sea south of Crete, so we sail instead sixty-five miles up the coast to Sidon. From there,

> we put out to sea and sailed under the shelter of Cyprus because the winds were contrary. And when we had sailed through the sea along the coast of Cilicia and Pamphylia, we landed at Myra in Lycia. And there the centurion found an Alexandrian ship sailing for Italy, and he put us aboard it. And when we had sailed slowly for a good many days, and with difficulty had arrived off Cnidus, since the wind did not permit us to go farther, we sailed under the shelter of Crete, off Salmone; and with difficulty sailing

3. Maps © 1986, 1988 are taken from the *Life Application Bible* © 1988, 1989, 1990, 1991 by Tyndale House Publishers, Inc., Wheaton, IL 60189. Used by permission. All rights reserved. *Life Application* is a trademark of Tyndale House Publishers, Inc.

past it we came to a certain place called Fair Havens, near which was the city of Lasea. (27:4–8)

Once in Fair Havens, all hope of reaching Italy this season is given up. The winds are too contrary and too much time has passed (v. 9). John Pollock explains:

> October 5 came and went, the Jewish Day of Atonement. . . . The "Dangerous Days," when navigation was feasible but risky, were slipping away. With November 11, all navigation would cease on the open sea because then the sun and stars might be overcast for days on end, with no opportunity for bearings; this, rather than the inevitable hazard of storms, was the factor that stopped sea traffic in winter.[4]

The decision facing the crew, then, is whether to winter in Fair Havens' unprotected harbor or risk pushing on to the safer port of Phoenix a little further down the coast of Crete. Paul warns against sailing any further, "Men, I perceive that the voyage will certainly be attended with damage and great loss, not only of the cargo and the ship, but also of our lives" (v. 10). The ship's pilot and captain disagree with him, however, and in the end convince Julius and a majority of the crew that they can make Phoenix (vv. 11–12). So,

> when a moderate south wind came up, supposing that they had gained their purpose, they weighed anchor and began sailing along Crete, close inshore. But before very long there rushed down from the land a violent wind, called Euraquilo; and when the ship was caught in it, and could not face the wind, we gave way to it, and let ourselves be driven along. And running under the shelter of a small island called Clauda,[5] we were scarcely able to get the ship's boat under control. (vv. 13–16)

The decision to sail quickly proves to be a bad one—but the worst is yet to come.

---

4. Pollock, The Apostle, p. 278.

5. In a marginal note, the NASB notes that some ancient manuscripts read "Cauda," and different Bible versions also use this variant.

Leaving the shelter of Cauda they were soon enduring the full agony of rough seas. Without much weight of sail "We were violently stormtossed"— bobbing about like a cork, with the spray and rain preventing fires, drenching supplies, clothes, everything above and below decks. . . . The heaving, slippery boards made any movement painful. Paul, Luke, the convicts now released from their irons, and every able-bodied man would take turns at the pumps, but with the seeping of water through strained timbers the level in the bilge rose remorsely [sic] and the ship settled lower. On the second day to lighten her, the captain ordered loose cargo jettisoned: all livestock and much else. On the third, he ordered overboard the spare tackle—cables, spars, anything not essential.[6]

"From then on," writes Luke, "since neither sun nor stars appeared for many days, and no small storm was assailing us, . . . all hope of our being saved was gradually abandoned" (v. 20).

Spiritual Anchors

The last and most precious cargo heaved overboard is the passenger and crew's hope. They have exhausted every means for saving the ship, but to no avail. Now they simply huddle together, drifting in their own despair. At that helpless moment, the apostle Paul stands and casts the spiritual anchors needed to secure the people's hope in the only sure place—the Lord (v. 21). Let's look at those anchors and see the safety they offered.

First, Paul tossed out the *anchor of God's presence*.

"And yet now I urge you to keep up your courage, for there shall be no loss of life among you, but only of the ship. For this very night an angel of the God to whom I belong and whom I serve stood before me, saying, 'Do not be afraid, Paul; you must stand before Caesar; and behold, God has granted you all those who are sailing with you.' Therefore, keep up your courage, men, for I believe God, that it will

6. Pollock, *The Apostle*, p. 280.

138

turn out exactly as I have been told. But we must run aground on a certain island." (vv. 22–26)

Twice the Apostle tells his shipmates not to be discouraged. Why? Because God is with them and He has promised not to let them perish. Nothing is more terrifying than facing danger alone. But with the realization of God's presence comes renewed confidence and courage.

Does the Lord's presence mean, then, that the storm will quickly end? Not necessarily. God didn't promise the storm would end, only that His stabilizing presence would see them through it. In fact, Luke tells us that it wasn't until the fourteenth night of the storm that the crew first got a glimpse of God's promised island (v. 27a).

> As we were being driven about in the Adriatic Sea, about midnight the sailors began to surmise that they were approaching some land. (v. 27b)

Land! The ship's crew springs into action. A sounding tells them they are now at twenty fathoms. Next it's fifteen, and some of the crew fear the ship will break apart on the rocks. So they let down the ship's smaller boat on the pretense of laying out anchors and try to escape. God's presence had brought them this far, but now they turn to themselves to handle the rest (vv. 28–30).

Paul, however, perceives the deserters' plan and quickly warns the centurion and his soldiers that "unless these men remain in the ship, you yourselves cannot be saved" (v. 31).

The sailors stay (v. 32).

Next, Paul casts the *anchor of practical encouragement.*

> And until the day was about to dawn, Paul was encouraging them all to take some food, saying, "Today is the fourteenth day that you have been constantly watching and going without eating, having taken nothing. Therefore I encourage you to take some food, for this is for your preservation; for not a hair from the head of any of you shall perish." And having said this, he took bread and gave thanks to God in the presence of all; and he broke it and began to eat. And all of them were encouraged, and they themselves also took food. And all of us in the ship were two hundred and seventy-six persons. (vv. 33–37)

139

It's an astounding scene: 276 sodden survivors calmly eating in the midst of a hurricane at sea! What has changed? Not their circumstances, but their attitude. Paul's continual and confident encouragement has brought about a whole new perspective, one that is firmly anchored by the Apostle's confident trust in the Lord.

Finally, Paul lowers the *anchor of absolute faith*. This anchor is one that's visible not only in Paul but also in all the other passengers. Luke tells us that "when day came,

> they could not recognize the land; but they did observe a certain bay with a beach, and they resolved to drive the ship onto it if they could. And casting off the anchors, they left them in the sea while at the same time they were loosening the ropes of the rudders, and hoisting the foresail to the wind, they were heading for the beach. (vv. 39–40)

Imagine it. Someone shouts, "Land ho!" and the captain says, "Great, let's hit it!" And they do, even though they can hardly see where they're going, because God promised they'd run aground on an island, and they're sure He's kept His word.

> Striking a reef where two seas met, they ran the vessel aground; and the prow stuck fast and remained immovable, but the stern began to be broken up by the force of the waves. (v. 41)

Abandoning Ship, Arriving Safely

Amidst the chaos of the roaring waves and the splintering stern, the crew and passengers quickly prepare to abandon ship. Before jumping overboard, however, the soldiers plan to kill all the prisoners, for according to Roman law, a guard would lose his life if he lost his prisoner (v. 42). So instead of risking any of them swimming away and escaping, they seek Julius' permission to slaughter the lot.

Fortunately, Julius opposes the plan and takes command, ordering those who could swim to

> jump overboard first and get to land, and the rest should follow, some on planks, and others on various things from the ship. And thus it happened that they all were brought safely to land. (vv. 43b–44)

Timeless Truths from a Shipwreck

Whew! We made it—hungry, seasick, soaked, and exhausted maybe, but we made it. But where to? This island littered with the flotsam of battered survivors isn't the bustling Rome God promised. We're not there yet, which raises an important question that perhaps crossed even Paul's mind as he numbly dragged himself onto the beach: Why are there shipwrecks when we're going in the right direction?

Since we all suffer shipwrecks, even when we're proceeding in our Father's will, this question is a universal one. So, to close our journey together, let's briefly note four reasons barriers occur when we're doing what is right.

First of all, there's satanic opposition. Ray Stedman, in his book *Acts 21–28: Triumphs of the Body*, writes:

> In Paul's letter to the Romans he said that he had tried many times to go to Rome and had been prevented, hindered. Paul always said it was Satan who had put those hindrances in his path. The enemy did not want Paul in Rome, for that was the strategic center of the empire and also the very headquarters of evil. Satan did not want this mighty apostle, coming in the strength and power of a risen Lord, to move into this city and start breaking down the strongholds of darkness by which Satan held in grip the entire civilized world. So Satan delayed Paul every way he could, fighting every step of the way.[7]

Even though satanic opposition is real, it's good to remember that nothing can touch a child of God that has not passed through His omniscient control. The Lord could have canceled Satan's plans to shipwreck Paul, but instead He allowed it. Why? Perhaps because He wanted to use Paul to witness to the 275 other people aboard that ship. Sometimes God allows shipwrecks so He can work through us. Imagine what impact Paul had on those soldiers, on Julius, and on the other passengers who knew nothing of the one true God.

Still another reason is to deepen our maturity. Perhaps there are

7. Ray Stedman, *Acts 21–28: Triumphs of the Body* (Santa Ana, Calif.: Vision House Publishers, 1981), p. 120.

lessons we need to learn that only shipwrecks can teach us. As strong in the faith as Paul was, perhaps there were still areas in his life that needed testing and proving.

Last, and possibly most realistically, nobody really knows *why* we get shipwrecked. Paul could have made the journey in a few weeks; instead, it took seven months! Why? The Scriptures don't say. Just as the Lord never explained to Job why He allowed Satan to shipwreck his life, so He doesn't always explain Himself to us either. The Bible's focus isn't on who causes pain or why it's allowed, but on our *response* to it. If your ship has been blown off course, what will you do now? That's the important question.

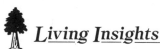 *Living Insights*

Do you know someone whose life has been recently shipwrecked? Perhaps a friend who has run aground on some intense suffering, or one who is foundering in deep waters of failure?

Debris from every kind of shipwreck is floating all around us—broken marriages, ruined relationships, shattered dreams, mangled morals, twisted guilt, damaged hearts. And the need is great for courageous Christians like Paul who will stand faithfully in life's uncertainty and proclaim the spiritual anchors that can hold people fast to Christ.

Is there a particular spiritual anchor from our lesson that someone near you needs right now? The reassuring anchor of God's presence, perhaps, or an anchor of practical encouragement?

Use the space provided to think carefully about this person's needs. How best can you minister to him or her?

_____

_____

_____

_____

 *Living Insights*

Why does God allow shipwrecks? Who knows all the reasons, really? And yet, if you look closely at Paul's shipwreck, you just might be able to see one that concerns a certain Roman centurion named Julius.

When we read the dramatic story in Acts 27, our attention naturally follows the plight of the main protagonist—Paul. Read the story again, however, and this time pay close attention to the subplot concerning Paul and Julius.

———◆———

Can you see any evidence that God may have used Paul in that crisis to draw Julius to Himself? For a clearer picture, take another look at the story in Acts 27, this time through just the highlights of Paul's interaction with the centurion.

• Julius takes custody of Paul as a prisoner (v. 1).

• Within a day, Paul has earned Julius' trust and is allowed to go ashore in Sidon to see friends (v. 3).

• When the dispute arose over whether to winter in Fair Havens or press on to Phoenix, the centurion respected Paul's judgment enough to allow him, a prisoner, to give his opinion (vv. 9–11).

• At the crisis point, when all hope of survival was given up, Julius allows Paul to stand and encourage the ship's company with the assurance of God's protective care (vv. 21–26).

• When the sailors tried to abandon ship and Paul told Julius that it would jeopardize the ship's safety, the centurion listened and immediately had them brought back on board (vv. 31–32).

• Julius gained encouragement from Paul and ate (vv. 33–36).

• Finally, when the soldiers planned to kill the prisoners, it was Julius who intervened and stopped them, specifically because he wanted Paul brought safely through (vv. 42–43).

Now can you see a reason, possibly, why God allowed that shipwreck, and maybe a reason, too, why He would allow a shipwreck in your life? If you're experiencing one right now, could it be that in your situation there's a Julius whom the Lord wants to reach through you?

Chapter 17

TIME TO HEAL
Acts 28:1–10

Henry Wadsworth Longfellow masterfully depicted the drama and tragedy of a shipwreck in his poem "The Wreck of the Hesperus."

> And ever the fitful gusts between
> A sound came from the land;
> It was the sound of the trampling surf
> On the rocks and the hard sea-sand.

> The breakers were right beneath her bows,
> She drifted a dreary wreck,
> And a whooping billow swept the crew
> Like icicles from her deck.

> She struck where the white and fleecy waves
> Looked soft as carded wool,
> But the cruel rocks, they gored her side
> Like the horns of an angry bull.

> Her rattling shrouds, all sheathed in ice,
> With the masts went by the board;
> Like a vessel of glass, she stove and sank,
> Ho! ho! the breakers roared![1]

Similarly, the angry surf pitched and crushed the ship that, on its way to Rome, had at last run aground on an island in the stormy Mediterranean Sea. As the waves battered the boat, the people on board swam or floated to shore, looking like so much human debris. Soaked, hungry, and shivering, they huddled together as they turned to watch the churning sea slowly dismantle their ship. Finally, "Like a vessel of glass, she stove and sank, Ho! ho! the breakers roared!"

However, everyone was safe, for God had brought them through the storm. And now, on this island still miles from Rome, God was going to give them time to heal.

1. Excerpted from Henry Wadsworth Longfellow's "The Wreck of the Hesperus," quoted in *A Treasury of the World's Best Loved Poems* (New York, N.Y.: Crown Publishers, Avenel Books, 1961), p. 133.

Initial Orientation

We learned from Luke's account of the shipwreck in Acts 27 that there had been 276 people on board the ship. They had all survived the storm and made it to land, but where were they? Luke, as a member of the stranded party, soon discovered the answer to that question:

> When [all the prisoners and crew] had been brought safely through, then we found out that the island was called Malta. (28:1)

Located about fifty miles south of Sicily, Malta is a rugged Mediterranean island some eighteen miles long and eight miles wide. In Paul's day, the island's name was actually Melita, which was

> the Canaanite word for "refuge." . . . It has even been suggested that what Luke means by saying, "then we knew that the island was called Melita," is "we recognized that it was well-named."[2]

Paul and company had literally arrived at an island of refuge, where they could recuperate from their near-death ordeal and prepare themselves to meet the coming challenges of Rome. But this healing process could not be accomplished overnight—even the father of medicine, Hippocrates, recognized that fact. "Healing is a matter of time," he once wrote, "but it is sometimes also a matter of opportunity."[3]

The amount of time God prescribed for Paul to heal was three months—the time it took for the weather to permit safe sailing (see v. 11). But the Apostle wasn't just sipping coconut juice under a palm; as we will see, he used his healing time as an opportunity to experience God's presence in new and refreshing ways—ways that revolved around his relationship with the islanders.

Personal Treatment

Luke calls the islanders "natives," or *barbaros* in Greek (v. 2a),

2. F. F. Bruce, Commentary on the Book of the Acts, The New International Commentary on the New Testament series (Grand Rapids, Mich.: William B. Eerdmans Publishing Co., 1954), p. 521.

3. Hippocrates, Precepts, as quoted in Bartlett's Familiar Quotations, 15th ed., rev. and enl., ed. Emily Morison Beck (Boston, Mass.: Little, Brown and Co., 1980), p. 79.

from which we get our word *barbarian*.[4] However, far from being crude or hostile, these local inhabitants were compassionate toward the shipwrecked passengers.

Extraordinary Kindness

> The natives showed us extraordinary kindness; for because of the rain that had set in and because of the cold, they kindled a fire and received us all. (v. 2)

To these waterlogged people who had just ridden a wind-whipped roller coaster for two weeks, how warm that fire must have felt—emotionally as well as physically! For them, the Maltese healing process had begun, as God was using the natives to meet the travelers' immediate needs.

Unjust Criticism

However, during any time of healing—whether we are recovering from depression, abuse, or some crisis—there is the danger of others misunderstanding our pain. This happens to Paul when he decides to help tend the fire.

> When Paul had gathered a bundle of sticks and laid them on the fire, a viper came out because of the heat, and fastened on his hand. And when the natives saw the creature hanging from his hand, they began saying to one another, "Undoubtedly this man is a murderer, and though he has been saved from the sea, justice has not allowed him to live." (vv. 3–4)

The islanders interpreted Paul's snakebite as divine retribution for the severest wrongdoing, murder. To them, his calamity was punishment and, therefore, proof of his guilt.

Job's counselors held that same assumption, didn't they? To them, Job's problems could only be a result of unconfessed sin (see Job 22). When calamity strikes our lives, others may tell us, "Obviously, God is disciplining you. Clean up your life before it's too late." But that advice is based on false theology. Snakebites don't prove wrongdoing, any more than hard times always imply hidden sin.

---

4. "To the Greek the barbarian was a man who said *bar-bar*, that is, a man who spoke an unintelligible foreign language and not the beautiful Greek tongue." William Barclay, *The Acts of the Apostles*, rev. ed., The Daily Study Bible Series (Philadelphia, Pa.: Westminster Press, 1976), p. 187.

When Paul doesn't die from the snakebite, the natives are amazed. "Maybe he's not a murderer," they whisper to each other. "But then again, maybe he's not . . . a man!"

Inappropriate Exaltation

> They were expecting that he was about to swell up or suddenly fall down dead. But after they had waited a long time and had seen nothing unusual happen to him, they changed their minds and began to say that he was a god. (Acts 28:6)

From a murderer to a god!

The people's opinion of Paul has swung from one extreme to the other. Paul, though, seems completely unaffected by their mistaken notion; Luke doesn't record a single word of response on his part. He just quietly goes about the business of resting and healing—which, interestingly, opens up some opportunities for God to use him in the healing of others.

Relational Concern

The first opportunity arises when a prominent Roman invites Paul and his companions for a visit.

Instant Healing

> Now in the neighborhood of that place were lands belonging to the leading man of the island, named Publius, who welcomed us and entertained us courteously three days. And it came about that the father of Publius was lying in bed afflicted with recurrent fever and dysentery; and Paul went in to see him and after he had prayed, he laid his hands on him and healed him. (vv. 7–8)

Paul demonstrates his authority as an apostle by miraculously and instantly healing Publius' father. Off to the side, though, Luke watches God work through Paul. As a physician, he is the logical one to tend the sick man, but he willingly gives Paul the lead. Soon, though, God would use Luke's skills, too, to help the people.

Prolonged Healing

> And after this had happened, the rest of the people

147

on the island who had diseases were coming to him and getting cured. (v. 9)

The Greek word for *healed* in verse 8 is *iaomai*; but in verse 9, Luke uses a different Greek word, *therapeuō*, from which we derive our word *therapy*—translated here as "cured." This word can mean "to treat medically."[5] It may infer that Luke was involved in Paul's healing ministry, perhaps by using natural means to cure the people rather than supernatural. Whatever the subtleties the word indicates, the end result was that the Lord was using Paul and Luke to minister to the physical needs of the people as a sign of His power and the truth of the gospel.

Practical Benefits

The islanders must have been amazed by these remarkable survivors, and they were also appreciative of their kindness toward them. Luke records that

> they also honored us with many marks of respect; and when we were setting sail, they supplied us with all we needed. (v. 10)

From when the passengers of the ship first blew onto the island to the time they sailed away, three months of healing had taken place—not only in the lives of Paul and his shipmates but also in the lives of the Maltese natives. Lingering in the Mediterranean trade winds are two lessons to remember during our own times of healing.

First, *the one who takes time to heal should be respected, not resented.* Although accusatory at first, the people respected Paul during his respite on the island. Concerning those we know who are recovering from emotional shipwrecks, we, too, must respect their needs and be patient with them during their sometimes tortuous road back to health.

Second, *the one who is healed will be better equipped to help others.* Enduring emotional storms and experiencing God's healing afterwards make us real to others. We can say honestly to people recovering from similar ordeals, "I know how you feel; God helped me through, and He can help you too."

---

5. Fritz Rienecker, *A Linguistic Key to the Greek New Testament,* ed. Cleon L. Rogers, Jr. (Grand Rapids, Mich.: Zondervan Publishing House, Regency Reference Library, 1980), p. 343.

Former baseball pitcher Dave Dravecky was thrown a curve one day by a man who thought he knew the reason for the cancer in Dave's pitching arm.

> I was in Grand Rapids, Michigan, speaking at a chapel service when I was approached by a man in his twenties. He told me I had cancer because there was sin in my life. He told me that the Holy Spirit revealed to him that God had a special plan for me — to be a preacher — but first I had to get rid of the sin.[6]

Just like the natives of Malta, the young man assumed that Dravecky's calamity was evidence of some guilt. But, like Paul's snakebite, his cancer was not a result of personal sin. If it was, what kind of God would we be serving?

> The issue is not *our* character but the character of God.
>
> Is God the kind of God who gives people tumors when they sin? Does he dole out diseases when we fail him? Say, maybe, cataracts when we lust or hardening of the arteries when we hate. Does he punish us with leukemia and muscular dystrophy and blindness?
>
> The Pharisees thought so. When they came across a blind man, they asked Jesus, "Who sinned, this man or his parents, that he was born blind?" Jesus responded by saying "neither," and then proceeded to heal the man.[7]

Psalm 103:10–14 describes that divine healing touch, portraying God's infinite compassion toward us in our sin. Take a moment right now to read those verses.

If you're suffering like Dave Dravecky or the Apostle Paul and someone has thrown you a curve, what comfort do these verses give you?

6. Dave and Jan Dravecky with Ken Gire, *When You Can't Come Back* (Grand Rapids, Mich.: Zondervan Publishing House; San Francisco, Calif.: HarperSanFrancisco, 1992), p. 72.

7. Dravecky, Dravecky, and Gire, *When You Can't Come Back*, p. 72.

_____

_____

_____

_____

Thinking about the image of God portrayed in Psalm 103, Dravecky adds:

> Is that the picture of a father who takes a belt to his children when they spill their milk or wet their pants? Is that the picture of a God who gives people cancer when they sin? I don't think so.
>
> I didn't get angry with the man. I felt sad that he was carrying around such a distorted picture of God. And I wondered how that picture would get him through life when one day he would have to walk through his own valley of suffering.[8]

Before you come to your valley of suffering, make sure your picture of God is true.

Living Insights   STUDY TWO

"What do you do for fun?" asked the wise doctor.

The visibly exhausted young mother had come to see him for physical, not social, advice. Surprised by his question, she glanced around the examining room and stammered, "What do you mean?"

"Fun . . . you know, hobbies, sports, recreation. Don't you do anything just to relax and enjoy yourself?"

She began, "Well, I . . . no that was years ago. Oh, I know, I . . . no, not anymore." Suddenly it occurred to her that, with the kids, work, the house, church, and all the other demands on her time, she didn't do anything for fun. Nothing. At that moment, her life tasted wretchedly bland.

Do you feel like this young mother? If so, somewhere in your life you need a Malta, an island of refuge.

---

8. Dravecky, Dravecky, and Gire, _When You Can't Come Back,_ p. 73.

If you had three hours per week of uninterrupted time for fun, restoration and refreshment, how would you spend it? Would you take dancing lessons? Ride a bike? Play a sport? Learn how to paint? What would you do?

The problem is, most of us feel these kinds of activities are selfish and un-Christian. Free time should be spent calling a needy friend, working at church, or reading our Bibles. We feel irresponsible if we take time to play. But play is important—it is our refuge from life's storms.

Because relaxation time is so valuable, we must plan it wisely. Where in your week can you carve out a few hours for restorative fun? What details do you need to work out? Make your plans specific.

You can't spend all your time on your island of refuge, but you can visit it regularly. How about this week?

Chapter 18

CHAINED ... BUT OFFERING FREEDOM

Acts 28:11–24

For years, Paul and the Christians in Rome were long-distance friends—sort of international pen pals. He had heard about them through mutual acquaintances and, in admiration of their courageous faith, wrote them a letter—his doctrinal masterpiece, The Epistle of Paul to the Romans.

More than just weighty doctrine, though, this letter expressed Paul's deep desire to someday meet his faraway friends, to live among them, to share their heartaches and joys. Lovingly, he wrote:

> For God, whom I serve in my spirit in the preaching of the gospel of His Son, is my witness as to how unceasingly I make mention of you, always in my prayers making request, if perhaps now at last by the will of God I may succeed in coming to you. For I long to see you in order that I may impart some spiritual gift to you, that you may be established; that is, that I may be encouraged together with you while among you, each of us by the other's faith, both yours and mine. (1:9–12)

After a harrowing journey on the high seas, Paul would finally meet them face-to-face. But Paul's circumstances had drastically changed since he had written his letter . . . he was a convict now. How could he pastor them as a prisoner? How could he touch their lives with chains on his wrists? It had been his dream to minister in Rome—but God had something different in mind than what Paul had expected.

Arrival: Destination Realized

In our last chapter, we left Paul and the others on Malta, the island of refuge, recuperating from their shipwreck experience. Now let's rejoin them as they complete their trip to Rome. Julius, the Roman centurion in charge, has booked our passage on a north-bound ship, and our friend Dr. Luke is keeping notes as we board

152

this new vessel and weigh anchor for Italy.

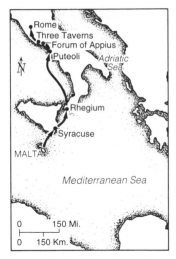

At the end of three months we set sail on an Alexandrian ship which had wintered at the island, and which had the Twin Brothers for its figure-head. And after we put in at Syracuse, we stayed there for three days. And from there we sailed around and arrived at Rhegium, and a day later a south wind sprang up, and on the second day we came to Puteoli. (Acts 28:11–13)

Paul Arrives in Rome[1]

The rhythmic rising and falling of the ship, the salty spray in our faces, and the spirited winds of spring confirm our good feelings about this leg of the voyage. With the storms of open sea behind us, we travel from harbor to harbor, coming closer and closer to Rome.

As we glide into the Gulf of Naples, which hugs the city of Puteoli, we thank God for the favorable winds and the progress we've made—almost two hundred miles in one day. Once in the bustling port city, we find some believers who invite us to stay a week with them until our trip resumes (v. 14a).[2] How warm their Christian hospitality feels to us, so far from home!

At the end of the week, Julius leads us with the other prisoners onto the Appian Way for the remaining hundred miles to Rome. Although we're traveling by land now, a sea of Roman faces seems to wash by us on this well-traveled highway. What will it be like in the city itself? What will the people be like there? What kind of justice will Paul receive? Will the Christians welcome us as the Puteolian believers did?

---

1. Maps ©1986, 1988 are taken from the *Life Application Bible* ©1988, 1989, 1990, 1991 by Tyndale House Publishers, Inc., Wheaton, IL 60189. Used by permission. All rights reserved. *Life Application* is a trademark of Tyndale House Publishers, Inc.

2. Although Paul was a prisoner, Julius allowed him the freedom to stay with these believers in Puteoli while the centurion attended to some official business in the city (compare with 27:3).

Our misgivings are soon quieted, for

> the brethren, when they heard about us, came from
> there as far as the Market of Appius and Three Inns
> to meet us; and when Paul saw them, he thanked
> God and took courage. (v. 15)

These believers had traveled from Rome to welcome us like dignitaries.[3] In their enthusiastic greeting, it is as if God is telling us, "I am alive in Rome, and I will take care of you!"

Encouraged despite his chains, Paul leads us the last few miles to the imperial city. As Luke concisely writes, after months of travel through raging seas and unknown lands, "Thus we came to Rome" (v. 14b).

Circumstance: Situation Determined

> And when we entered Rome, Paul was allowed
> to stay by himself, with the soldier who was guarding
> him. (v. 16)

Although Luke tells just the facts, his narrative resonates with mixed emotion. Finally, Paul is in Rome—a city of one million people who have never heard the hope and promise of Christ. Yet he is confined to his apartment and leashed to a Roman guard. This is not exactly the situation he had in mind when he first dreamed of going to Rome.

For two years, he would be restricted to this room (v. 30). How he must have longed for just one day's freedom to proclaim Christ to the milling crowds in the local marketplace, as he had done in the cities of Asia and Greece. God, however, had other plans for the spread of the gospel.

Ministry: Evangelism Applied

Amazingly, God intends to use the limitations of the situation itself as a platform for the gospel; Paul's chains will be the medium for God's message of freedom.

Interesting Facts

Let's take a look at three of the limitations that Paul turned

---

3. Three Inns was about thirty miles from Rome, and ten miles farther down the Appian Way was the Market of Appius.

into opportunities. First, since Paul can't go to the people with the gospel, the people come to him.

> And it happened that after three days he called together those who were the leading men of the Jews. (v. 17a)

Whenever Paul came to a new city, his habit had been to preach to the Jews in the local synagogue. In Rome, however, he has to invite the Jews to his apartment, and they willingly come to listen to him.

Second, since he can't unchain himself, he uses his situation as an object lesson. We can imagine him pondering how to teach believers about spiritual warfare. Glancing around the room, he suddenly focuses on the Roman soldier sitting a few feet away . . . *that's it!* Then he pens the priceless words of Ephesians 6: "Put on the full armor of God. . . ."

Besides Ephesians, he'll write three other influential letters from this apartment: Philippians, Colossians, and Philemon. Indeed, Paul is making the best of a bad circumstance, as James Stalker observed:

> He would have liked to be moving from synagogue to synagogue in the immense city, preaching in its streets and squares, and founding congregation after congregation among the masses of its population. Another man, thus arrested in a career of ceaseless movement and immured within prison walls, might have allowed his mind to stagnate in sloth and despair. But Paul behaved very differently. Availing himself of every possibility of the situation, he converted his one room into a center of far-reaching activity and beneficence. On the few square feet of space allowed him he erected a fulcrum with which he moved the world, establishing within the walls of Nero's capital a sovereignty more extensive than his own.[4]

The third converted limitation is this: since he can't change what others are saying about him, he simply tells the truth. He can't alter the charges made against him by the Jews in Caesarea, but he

---

4. James Stalker, *The Life of St. Paul* (New York, N.Y.: Fleming H. Revell Co., 1950), p. 136.

can explain the truth to the Jews in Rome as they gather at his door. "Brethren," he addresses them,

> "though I had done nothing against our people, or the customs of our fathers, yet I was delivered prisoner from Jerusalem into the hands of the Romans. And when they had examined me, they were willing to release me because there was no ground for putting me to death. But when the Jews objected, I was forced to appeal to Caesar; not that I had any accusation against my nation. For this reason therefore, I requested to see you and to speak with you, for I am wearing this chain for the sake of the hope of Israel." And they said to him, "We have neither received letters from Judea concerning you, nor have any of the brethren come here and reported or spoken anything bad about you." (vv. 17b–21)

Apparently, somewhere between Palestine and Rome, God had withered the gossip grapevine the Jews in Jerusalem and Asia had tended carefully for more than two years. As a result, these Jews in Rome are open to hearing Paul's words. And they're curious! What do his chains have to do with "the hope of Israel"? Look at their response:

> "We desire to hear from you what your views are; for concerning this sect, it is known to us that it is spoken against everywhere." (v. 22)

Christianity is receiving bad press in Rome, but through his situation, Paul can set the record straight when they come back a second time.

Unique Approach

Without having to leave his apartment—which he can't do anyway—Paul just patiently waits as the Jews make all the arrangements for him to preach.

> When they had set a day for him, they came to him at his lodging in large numbers; and he was explaining to them by solemnly testifying about the kingdom of God, and trying to persuade them concerning Jesus, from both the Law of Moses and from the

Prophets, from morning until evening. (v. 23)

Isn't that great? Although Paul is caged and chained, God still provides him a way to proclaim the gospel to a large crowd.[5] In our lives, we sometimes think God can't use us because we feel chained by a physical problem or confined by a situation that is out of our control. But it's in those times of weakness and limitation that God ministers most effectively through us . . . if we depend on Him.

Paul himself best expressed this truth in one of his letters to the Corinthian believers:

> And He has said to me, "My grace is sufficient for you, for power is perfected in weakness." Most gladly, therefore, I will rather boast about my weaknesses, that the power of Christ may dwell in me. Therefore I am well content with weaknesses, with insults, with distresses, with persecutions, with difficulties, for Christ's sake; for when I am weak, then I am strong. (2 Cor. 12:9–10)

Because Paul was content with his weaknesses, he was free from bitterness toward those who had put him in chains. Ironically, it was those chains that were giving him a forum for the gospel—the very truth his enemies hated!

Typical Response

As Paul proclaimed the hope of Israel to the many Jews gathered around his small apartment, he must have longed for each one of them to embrace Jesus as their Messiah and Savior. Luke reports,

> Some were being persuaded by the things spoken, but others would not believe. (Acts 28:24)

God had overcome the incredible limitations of Paul's imprisonment in order for these people to hear the liberating truth of the gospel. And although many still did not unlock their hearts and receive Christ, some did become Christians. How that must have thrilled Paul! His hands may have been chained and his freedom removed, but as long as he kept depending on the Lord day by day, nothing could manacle his voice and the gospel he proclaimed.

---

5. Paul proclaimed the gospel by explaining, testifying, and persuading. In so doing, he was appealing to the listener's total being—intellect, emotions, and will.

🌲 *Living Insights*

One modern-day model of faith in the midst of limitations is Joni Eareckson Tada. After a diving accident that left her paralyzed from the neck down, she struggled with questions about her purpose and her relationship with God. But God showed her, as He did with Paul, that His grace would see her through.

> Can God still use me, paralyzed? Can I, paralyzed, still worship God and love Him? He has taught me that I can.
>
> Maybe God's gift to me is my dependence on Him. I will never reach the place where I'm self-sufficient, where God is crowded out of my life. I'm aware of His grace to me every moment.[6]

You may not be confined to a wheelchair because of paralysis, but perhaps there are other limitations that you think are restricting your service for the Lord. Maybe, in your life, you've sensed God opening Rome's door—a place where there is great potential for the gospel. But you've resisted, saying, "I can't do that, not in these chains!"

In spite of Paul's chains, God brought the people to him to hear the gospel. In spite of Joni's paralysis, God has used her wheelchair as a platform for worldwide ministry. How might God use your limitation to enrich your service for Him? You can find out as you release any self-sufficiency that crowds God out and depend on His grace to you every moment.

🌲 *Living Insights*

While imprisoned in Rome, Paul wrote to the concerned believers in Philippi:

> Now I want you to know, brethren, that my circumstances have turned out for the greater progress of the gospel. (Phil. 1:12)

6. Joni Eareckson Tada, as quoted by Philip Yancey in *Where Is God When It Hurts?* (Grand Rapids, Mich.: Zondervan Publishing House, 1977), pp. 119–20.

In light of what we now know about Paul's situation, it's amazing that he could make this statement. But take a look at Philippians 1:13–14. In what ways did his imprisonment enhance and not impede the progress of the gospel?

_____

_____

_____

Paul's attitude during his imprisonment was instrumental in turning his limitations into victories for Christ. What features of his attitude do you notice in verses 15–21?

_____

_____

_____

_____

In what ways can you adopt Paul's attitude in relation to a current negative situation you are facing?

_____

_____

_____

A. W. Tozer penned a prayer that may echo your commitment to Christ in your present circumstances. Claim it as your own as you read it to the Lord.

> Lord, I would trust Thee completely; I would be altogether Thine; I would exalt Thee above all. I desire that I may feel no sense of possessing anything outside of Thee. I want constantly to be aware of Thy overshadowing Presence and to hear Thy speaking Voice. I long to live in restful sincerity of heart. I want to live so fully in the Spirit that all my thought may be as sweet incense ascending to Thee and every act of my life may be an act of worship.

Therefore I pray in the words of Thy great servant of old, "I beseech Thee so for to cleanse the intent of mine heart with the unspeakable gift of Thy grace, that I may perfectly love Thee and worthily praise Thee." And all this I confidently believe Thou wilt grant me through the merits of Jesus Christ Thy Son. Amen.[7]

7. A. W. Tozer, *The Pursuit of God* (Wheaton, Ill.: Tyndale House Publishers, n.d.), p. 128.

Chapter 19

THE END OF THE BEGINNING

Acts 28:23–31

The November darkness cloaking London in 1942 seemed heavier than ever. Hitler's Luftwaffe had invaded English skies, and all Britain was feeling the dread of his enlarging shadow. Frequently now, air raid sirens would shatter the blacked-out nights as well as the frayed nerves of the people, who would scramble in numb fear to the shelters. Then, the bombs would come—whistle, boom, whistle . . . boom, boom, boom—as the Britishers clung to one another through the night.

How long could they endure this unrelenting darkness?

Prime Minister Winston Churchill wished he could answer that question. What could he say to steel the people's melting courage? On November 10, he addressed a worried audience at the Lord Mayor's Day Luncheon, slowly growling these immortal words:

> Now this is not the end. It is not even the beginning
> of the end. But it is, perhaps, the end of the beginning.[1]

How appropriately these lines fit the final verses of the book of Acts. The church's beginning, with its setbacks and struggles, is ending—but by no means has its story ended. As Christ has promised, "I will build My church; and the gates of Hades shall not overpower it" (Matt. 16:18b). And today, with hell still pummeling the church with bombs of criticism and hatred, the war is nowhere near over . . . and will not be until Christ prevails.

In his description of Paul's Roman ministry at the end of Acts 28, Luke paints for us a wartime portrait of our Christian battle. Sometimes there is victory, often there is defeat, but always there is hope—the hope to which we cling, for which we fight, and with which we will someday win.

---

1. Winston Churchill, as quoted in *Bartlett's Familiar Quotations*, 15th ed., rev. and enl., ed. Emily Morison Beck (Boston, Mass.: Little, Brown and Co., 1980), p. 746.

161

Declaration of the Gospel

Initially, the Apostle's ministry in Rome targeted the Jewish populace—he had already spoken to "the leading men of the Jews" (vv. 17–22). Unlike the Jews in Asia and Jerusalem, these Roman Jews were open to his ideas and wanted to hear him further, so

> when they had set a day for him, they came to him at his lodging in large numbers; and he was explaining to them by solemnly testifying about the kingdom of God, and trying to persuade them concerning Jesus, from both the Law of Moses and from the Prophets, from morning until evening. (v. 23)

Within the "comfort" of his house arrest, Paul sets forth the truth that has had such an irrevocable effect on his life—an effect he wouldn't trade for all the freedom the world could offer. How does he go about telling his message?

Method and Message

Paul has a threefold method of communication: "explaining," "testifying," and "persuading" (see v. 23). The Greek word for *explaining* means "to lay out, to set forth."[2] Luke used it in 11:4 to describe how Peter explained to the Jews "in orderly sequence" his vision of the sheet of unclean animals. Later, Aquila and Priscilla pulled Apollos aside and "explained to him the way of God more accurately" (18:26). With these two contexts in mind, we can conclude that Paul explained his message by laying out arguments accurately and in a logical order—an ideal we can strive for when we are on the front lines explaining God's truths.

Second, Paul is "testifying"—a word in Greek that means "to declare emphatically."[3] We can imagine him pacing as he makes a key point, then standing square-shouldered as he resists a scoffer, or sitting on the edge of his seat as he focuses on a receptive listener. From morning until evening, he is passionately engaged in a verbal battle for the people's souls.

---

2. Fritz Rienecker, *A Linguistic Key to the Greek New Testament*, ed. Cleon L. Rogers, Jr. (Grand Rapids, Mich.: Zondervan Publishing House, Regency Reference Library, 1980), p. 345.

3. H. Strathmann, *Theological Dictionary of the New Testament*, ed. Gerhard Kittel, trans. and ed. Geoffrey W. Bromiley (1967; reprint, Grand Rapids, Mich.: William B. Eerdmans Publishing Co., 1973), vol. 4, p. 511.

Third, his goal is to "persuade" them to respond to what he is saying; he is not just going through an academic exercise—he wants to effect a change. And because his arguments are based on evidence "from both the Law of Moses and from the Prophets," his words are particularly effective with this Jewish audience.[4]

The subject of his message was twofold: the kingdom of God and Jesus' mission.[5] He probably portrayed these themes in this way: God is sovereign ruler over the universe; but through Satan's deception, man revolted against the divine King. So God sent Jesus, the Messiah Prince, into the world to atone for sin and win back His wayward subjects. Now, through our faith in Christ, He can deliver us

> from the domain of darkness, and [transfer] us to the kingdom of His beloved Son. (Col. 1:13)

As Paul sketches out these truths, he accentuates them with evidence from his palette of Old Testament knowledge. By the end of the day, he has created a mural of Christ—His mission, His agony, and His glory. Will the people believe?

Response

Their response is typical of Paul's audiences throughout his ministry.

> Some were being persuaded by the things spoken, but others would not believe. (Acts 28:24)

The imperfect tenses of the Greek verbs suggest that some were beginning to believe but others continued to disbelieve.[6] Inevitably, an argument between these two groups erupts, for "they did not agree with one another" (v. 25a). And as they get caught up in their disagreement, they start to leave. With the tension mounting, how will Paul react?

Reaction to the Jews

Unlike Paul, we might have attempted to nervously pacify the crowd, saying, "Fellas, let's be friends and just agree to disagree."

---

4. For an example of how Paul probably preached Christ to the Jews using Old Testament passages, see 13:16–41.

5. According to verse 23, Paul explained and testified concerning the kingdom of God, but his method shifted to persuasion when he spoke to them about Jesus.

6. Rienecker, *Linguistic Key*, p. 345.

After all, the Jews had a powerful lobby in Rome, and we wouldn't want to get on their bad side.

However, their explosive response is not a surprise to Paul. For Jesus Himself had said:

> "Do not think that I came to bring peace on the earth; I did not come to bring peace, but a sword. For I came to set a man against his father, and a daughter against her mother, and a daughter-in-law against her mother-in-law; and a man's enemies will be the members of his household." (Matt. 10:34–36)

Because of the black-and-white nature of the gospel, Paul knows that conflict is inevitable. So, while the friction between the factions heats up, rather than ignoring the spiritual battle, he goes back to the foundation of the Scriptures to mark where the people stand:[7]

> "The Holy Spirit rightly spoke through Isaiah the prophet to your fathers, saying,
>
>> 'Go to the people and say,
>> "You will keep on hearing, but will not understand;
>> And you will keep on seeing, but will not perceive;
>> For the heart of this people has become dull,
>> And with their ears they scarcely hear,
>> And they have closed their eyes;
>> Lest they should see with their eyes,
>> And hear with their ears,
>> And understand with their heart and return,
>> And I should heal them.""'
>
> (Acts 28:25b–27)

And because most of these Jews are responding as stubbornly as the Israelites in Isaiah's day, Paul somberly adds,

> "Let it be known to you therefore, that this salvation of God has been sent to the Gentiles; they will also listen." (v. 28)

---

7. The power of Paul's message was not his brilliant logic or oratory skills but his consistent use of the Word of God—the foundation and zenith, the beginning and end of any ministry.

With that, the Jews take their leave, many of them angered but some of them convicted by this new teaching (v. 29).[8]

Actually, though, the teaching was not new. Announcing God's worldwide offer of salvation had been Paul's *raison d'etre* since his conversion. Today countless people have benefited from Paul's work to "bear [Jesus'] name before the Gentiles and kings and the sons of Israel" (9:15b) . . . including most of us.

Conclusion of the Book

In the last two verses of Acts, Luke adds the finishing touches to his wartime portrait. In so doing, he doesn't fill in the specifics about the Christians in Rome or Paul's trial and eventual death. However, he does paint a scene of a balanced, open, and hopeful ministry that we can emulate.

Universal Acceptance

> And [Paul] stayed two full years in his own rented quarters, and was welcoming all who came to him. (28:30)

Paul's door was open to anyone—rich or poor, Jew or Gentile, free or slave. Sometimes, though, we fall into the trap of excluding others because they're different from us, and we reflect the following attitude:

> Believe as I believe, no more, no less;
> That I am right, and no one else, confess;
> Feel as I feel, think only as I think;
> Eat what I eat, and drink but what I drink;
> Look as I look, do always as I do;
> And then, and only then, I'll fellowship with you.[9]

But how will people hear about Christ if we act this way? Let's open our doors and welcome people into our churches, our homes, and our lives.

---

8. Verse 29 tells us that they "departed, having a great dispute among themselves." But because many Greek manuscripts do not contain this verse and it repeats the information in verse 25, it is probably a copyist's addition to the text.

9. Leslie B. Flynn, *When the Saints Come Storming In* (Wheaton, Ill.: Scripture Press Publications, Victor Books, 1988), pp. 79–80.

Solid Content

In addition to welcoming the people, Paul was "preaching the kingdom of God, and teaching concerning the Lord Jesus Christ" (v. 31a). The message of Paul's life boiled down to these two themes. If a shopkeeper came to see him, he talked about how they related to business; if a mother, how they applied to the family; if a philosopher, how they defined all of human existence. Boil down the message of your life . . . do you find Christ and His kingdom there?

Nondefensive Style

As people came to Paul, he was preaching and teaching "with all openness, unhindered" (v. 31b). Since neither the Romans nor the Jews were hindering the gospel, he could be boldly open. He didn't have to guard his words, afraid that people were going to attack him. Instead, he could be vulnerable and warm, helping others come to know his Lord.

Final Comments

As we reflect on Luke's picture of Paul's ministry in Rome, we can define two characteristics which ought to mark our churches today.

First, *the church's message is positive and broad, not negative and exclusive.* This was Jesus' ideal for His church back at the beginning of Acts, when He commissioned the small band of Jewish Christians to spread His light to other Jews, Samaritans, and even pagan Gentiles (1:8). Now *we* have His light, given us to shine in people's darkness. It is a positive message, full of hope and freedom, not just a set of do's and don'ts. And it is a broad message, appealing to everyone, regardless of a person's appearance or background.

Second, *the church's method is active and relevant, not passive and dated.* From his small apartment, Paul was leading a revolution without swords or spears, but with the truths of the kingdom of God and the words of Christ—weapons that never rust or become obsolete. And he has passed them on to equip us for battle in our own spiritually war-torn world. How will we use them? Will we bury them in yesterday's formulas and creeds? Or will we unsheathe them to attack the problems and challenges of the present and future?

The world says we need a new, man-centered gospel to save us from society's ills. But only Christ can shine a ray of hope into the darkness of our times. Certainly, one day His full light will come, for as the angel announced to the disciples staring up into the sky,

"This Jesus, who has been taken up from you into heaven, will come in just the same way as you have watched Him go into heaven." (1:11b)

Until that day, let us press on and bear the good news of the Lord Jesus Christ, unashamed, unafraid, and unhindered.

🌲 Living Insights   STUDY ONE

Pastor Lloyd John Ogilvie gives us a window on our lives through the portholes of that grand old ocean liner, the *Queen Mary*.

> I can remember admiring the gallant determination with which the historic craft cut through the high waves. . . . As I walked on deck I would try to recapture the feeling of what it must have been like aboard the "Mary" as a lovely pleasure vessel and then as a troop ship carefully evading the German submarines. . . .
>
> The next time I saw the *Queen Mary* was as a museum piece, docked in the Long Beach harbor. Her last voyage had been around the world and then into the harbor, where she was stripped of her vitals. The gigantic engine had been removed as well as most of the sailing equipment. She sat there motionless, attached tightly to the dock. Shops now line the decks to sell souvenirs to visitors. The dining and lounge areas provide meeting places for groups and the cabins have been refurbished as hotel rooms for conventions. Actors have been hired to act out the parts of officers and crew with carefully studied British accents. The one thing the *Queen Mary* can't do now is to fulfill the reason for which she was built: to sail the high sea. I couldn't help feeling disappointed. Everything was the same, yet nothing was the same. The vessel had become a monument to past glory.[10]

10. Lloyd John Ogilvie, *Drumbeat of Love* (Waco, Tex.: Word Books, Publishers, 1976), pp. 281–82.

In your Christian life, do you ever feel like the *Queen Mary*, once active and effective for Christ but now lashed to the dock of routine? Stripped of her engines, the *Mary* will never sail again, but as a Christian, God's power will always be within you. As we observed in the last section of Acts, Paul fueled his ministry in three ways:

- he welcomed all who came to him,

- he talked about the kingdom of God and Jesus' mission, and

- he was boldly open with others.

In what ways can you begin emulating these characteristics?

_____

_____

_____

_____

_____

_____

You may be limited like Paul, who was restricted to his quarters, but your limitations don't have to tie down your witness for Christ. Cast off into God's adventuresome high seas, and start fulfilling once again the reason for which you were created.

🌳 *Living Insights* STUDY TWO

The book of Acts began with Jesus "speaking of the things concerning the kingdom of God" (1:3b), and it ended with Paul "preaching the kingdom of God, and teaching concerning the Lord Jesus Christ" (28:31). In the verses between, Luke chronicled what happened when those fireworks of truth exploded in the world. What could happen in your world if you began speaking about and living in the light of Jesus Christ and the kingdom of God?

Let's examine the implications. Broadly speaking, the kingdom of God is the realm where God is king, where His laws are followed and His privileges enjoyed. What would your home be like if you announced one day, "This is God's kingdom"? How would that affect what you say at home? What you see on television? The atmosphere you create?

_____

_____

What would your workplace be like if you made the same announcement? What changes would occur?

_____

_____

What would your church be like if you made that announcement? How would your perspective toward church change?

_____

_____

If Jesus Christ became more the focus of your thoughts and conversations, how would your attitudes change?

_____

_____

How would your perspective toward your enemies change?

_____

_____

What changes in behavior would others notice about you?

_____

_____

Today, the Acts story can be repeated over and over again in the lives of those who see and hear Christ's kingdom in you. It's what being His witness "in Jerusalem, and in all Judea and Samaria, and even to the remotest part of the earth" is all about.

Digging Deeper

Luke's conclusion of Acts leaves us wondering what happened to Paul after his two-year house arrest. From tradition and certain references in his letters, we can piece together a probable ending to the great Apostle's life.

In answer to the many prayers for his deliverance (see Phil. 1:19), the Roman court probably acquitted him around A.D. 62. Now free, he may have taken the opportunity to fulfill his long-held dream to preach Christ in Spain (see Rom. 15:28). He might also have visited his friend Philemon in Colossae as he had promised in Philemon 22. Despite having told the Ephesian elders that he would not see them again, it's possible that he would have stopped by Ephesus and commissioned Timothy as the church's pastor (see 1 Tim. 1:3). We know he traveled through Macedonia, writing his first letter to Timothy and taking Titus to Crete, where he left him to organize that island's ministry (Titus 1:5). From Crete, he would have sailed to Greece and written his letter to Titus while planning to winter in Nicopolis (3:12).

In A.D. 64, however, Nero suddenly slammed shut the door of religious freedom. Insane and infamously cruel, he blamed the Christians for the terrible fire in Rome that he himself had ordered. A vicious persecution of believers soon ignited, and Paul was probably arrested and dragged to Rome as a prisoner.

As a Roman citizen, the Apostle was allowed his day in court. Deserted by most of his supporters and falsely accused by his enemies, Paul had little hope of a second acquittal (see 2 Tim. 4:9–18). Tradition records that he was eventually sentenced to the horrible Mamertine prison, and it was here that he was beheaded. Dying alone and as a criminal, he became like his Lord even in death; indeed, he had surrendered everything to serve Christ. In return, as F. B. Meyer wrote,

> What a festal welcome he must have received [in heaven] from thousands whom he had turned from darkness to light, from the power of Satan unto God, and who were now to become his crown of rejoicing in the presence of the Lord! These from the highland of Galatia, and those from the seaboard of Asia Minor. These from Judaistic prejudice, and those from the depths of Gentile depravity and sin.

These from the degraded slave populations, and those from the ranks of the high-born and educated. Nor have such greetings ceased; but through all the centuries that have succeeded there are comparatively few that have passed along "the Way to the Celestial City" who have not had to acknowledge a deep debt of gratitude to him who, of all others, was enabled to give a clearer apprehension of the Divine method of justifying and saving sinners.[11]

11. F. B. Meyer, *Paul: More Than Conqueror* (Westchester, Ill.: Good News Publishers, 1959), p. 64.

Chapter 20

WHAT PLEASES GOD?

Selected Scripture

W hew! Our journey through the Acts of the Apostles has come to an end. Before moving on, though, let's take a moment to kick off our sandals, wiggle our toes, and settle into some final thoughts about our trip.

Do you remember where we began? We were in Jerusalem, standing beside Jesus. Our heads were still spinning from His recent death and resurrection when He led us up this mountain. Suddenly, He started ascending into heaven! But before He left, He promised to give us the Holy Spirit and the power to be His witnesses to the world. *Us* . . . imagine that!

Then the Holy Spirit came, and off we went throughout Jerusalem with Peter and Stephen. Persecuted, we fled with Philip to Samaria and Judea. A certain pharisee named Saul kept pursuing us, but he was stopped by Jesus on the road to Damascus and in a radical turnaround became Paul, Christ's champion witness. Holding high the flame of Christ, Paul took us to the faraway lands of Asia, Europe, and eventually the center of the ancient world, Rome.

It was all very exciting—but not without its challenges. For before we said good-bye to Paul, he pressed something into our hands . . . the same torch he himself had been carrying. Now we must carry Christ's flame from Jerusalem and Samaria to the remotest part of our world.

How are we to do this? We're not Paul. We don't have his gifts or determination—does God want us to witness for Christ just like he did? Do we have to be supersaints in order to carry Christ's flame to others? When it comes to being an effective Christian today, what does God expect?

Guidelines to Pleasing God

Essentially, God is looking for hearts that are tender toward Him, hearts that are eager to please Him rather than themselves or others. Jesus Himself is our model of the tender heart God is looking

This message was not a part of the original series but is compatible with it.

172

for. Speaking to a group of Pharisees—people who definitely did not please God—Jesus said:

> "When you lift up the Son of Man, then you will know that I am He, and I do nothing on My own initiative, but I speak these things as the Father taught Me. And He who sent Me is with Me; He has not left Me alone, for I always do the things that are pleasing to Him." (John 8:28–29)

From His words about Himself we can see into His soul, and there we find a beautiful submissiveness to the Father. If we'll take that attitude into our hearts as well, our actions, too, will please God.

Pleasing God Is Linked to Our Walk

It's our actions, the practical outworkings of our beliefs, that please God, because they provide the visible evidence of Christ in our lives. That's why Paul encouraged the Thessalonian believers to press on in their Christian walk:

> Finally then, brethren, we request and exhort you in the Lord Jesus, that, as you received from us instruction as to how you ought to walk and please God (just as you actually do walk), that you may excel still more. (1 Thess. 4:1)

What are some specific areas we can work on? Well first, our attitudes. Then how we respond to others, how we deal with irritations, how we bear disappointments, how well we resist the flesh. Each of these can reveal whether our walk with Christ is firm or faltering and whether we're truly seeking to please God.

Pleasing God Is Linked to Our Obedience

John admonishes us, "Let us not love with word or with tongue, but in deed and truth" (1 John 3:18). It's not our talk that ultimately pleases God, it's our deeds. And those deeds grow out of a heart that is determined to obey Christ's commandments. John continues,

> Beloved, if our heart does not condemn us, we have confidence before God; and whatever we ask we receive from Him, because we keep His commandments and do the things that are pleasing in His sight. (vv. 21–22)

One man who did "the things that are pleasing in His sight" was Enoch. Remember him? He never died; instead, at age 365, God took him straight to heaven (Gen. 5:21–24). Why did He do that? Because, according to the writer to the Hebrews, Enoch "was pleasing to God" (Heb. 11:5b). With a tender spirit, he obeyed God day after day because he cared about the things on God's heart.

How's your Christian walk, your path of obedience going right now? Would you say that you truly desire, like Christ, to do nothing from your own initiative? Do you "always do the things that are pleasing to Him?"

For most of us the answer is, probably not. But there's good news! God doesn't expect perfect torchbearers—if that was what He wanted, Christ would never have passed the flame to Paul and then to us! However, He does want us to guard against the things that can douse that flame and prevent us from burning true and steady for Him.

What Doesn't Please God

Although God loves us unconditionally, it's certainly possible for us to anger or disappoint Him. How? First, *an absence of faith* hinders us from pleasing God. "Without faith," the writer to the Hebrews declares, "it is impossible to please Him" (11:6a). We can't please God if we constantly worry about tomorrow and all it might or might not bring, because God wants to be trusted, and He wants the world to see the peace He offers to those who have faith in Him.

Second, *the activity of the flesh* is a roadblock to pleasing God. Paul stated this plainly: "Those who are in the flesh cannot please God" (Rom. 8:8). Fleshly activities, by definition, put self in place of God. When we pursue them, we want our way, our pleasure, and our glory. Thankfully, God has placed His Spirit within us to win over our flesh so that His will can become ours.

Third, *being a people-pleaser* sidetracks us from pleasing God. If the thrust of our lives is to impress others, then we won't be impressing God. Paul addressed the Galatian believers on this point:

> For am I now seeking the favor of men, or of God? Or am I striving to please men? If I were still trying to please men, I would not be a bond-servant of Christ. (Gal. 1:10)

Fourth, *meaningless religious externals* don't please God. The prophet Micah saw the Israelites mistakenly trying to win God's favor by using religious rituals, so he asked rhetorically:

> With what shall I come to the Lord
> And bow myself before the God on high?
> Shall I come to Him with burnt offerings,
> With yearling calves?
> Does the Lord take delight in thousands of rams,
> In ten thousand rivers of oil?
> Shall I present my first-born for my rebellious acts,
> The fruit of my body for the sin of my soul?
> (Mic. 6:6–7)

What does please God? Will giving all our money make Him happy? Going to church every Sunday for the rest of our lives? Offering all our free time for worthy causes? Sacrificing our children on the altar of our religious busy work? Surely there's a better way.

What Does Please God?

Ready for Micah's answer? It may surprise you.

> He has told you, O man, what is good;
> And what does the Lord require of you
> But to do justice, to love kindness,
> And to walk humbly with your God?
> (v. 8)

God's requirements are simple—so simple we often miss them. Let's take a closer look at each one.

Do What Is Right

To "do justice" is, in essence, to do what is right. Most of us know what is right because God has communicated it in His Word. However, *doing* what is right is another matter. Being honest, maintaining integrity, treating others fairly and impartially, using our power correctly—these are the right things to do.

Love What Is Kind

Kindness is rare in our world. Anger, self-absorption, rudeness, and hostility have become commonplace and inescapable—from the mall to the freeway, from the Department of Motor Vehicles to overcrowded subways.

So to love kindness means that we're going to stand out. Others may think we're weak because we don't step on people to get what we want. But in God's eyes, having compassion is a mark of strength; and it pleases Him very much.

Believe What Is True

The third trait which pleases God is a humble walk with Him—and believing that what He tells us is true. Because if we don't, if instead we believe the lies Satan circulates in our culture, we rationalize sin, defame God's character, and water down Christ's atonement. His delight, though, is when we meditate on His truth and hold it out like a life preserver in the world's stormy seas.

A Final Thought

Carrying on the work Paul and the other apostles began in the book of Acts is not as complicated as it seems. We sometimes think that it requires seminary training and at least ten years' church experience, but that is not true. Micah summed it up for us; Jesus lived it out for us. And His Spirit is still here to help us today.

> Through Him then, let us continually offer up a sacrifice of praise to God, that is, the fruit of lips that give thanks to His name. And do not neglect doing good and sharing; for with such sacrifices God is pleased. (Heb. 13:15–16)

 *Living Insights* STUDY ONE

Who in the world is Butch Wickensheimer? You've probably never heard of him, but if there was a "Torchbearers for Christ Hall of Fame," he'd be in it.

A baseball newcomer on the lowest rung of the minor leagues, he was playing for the Clinton, Iowa, Class A club. Like every minor league player, he dreamed of making it to the big leagues. Also on his mind, though, was serving Christ no matter what happened along his hopeful path to the majors.

One of his teammates noticed his obedient walk with the Lord.

> He intrigued me. When the rest of us were out having a good time, he was relaxing, reading his Bible,

176

staying sober. A nice guy. We kidded him about being religious, but he wasn't obnoxious about it. He didn't condemn anybody or corner them and preach at them. He just didn't let them interfere with his own convictions. On the team bus, he would try to sit under a light that was working so he could read his Bible.

I asked him what he saw in it. "Everything," he told me. "It's God's gift to man. It tells how much He loves us and how we can know Him."[1]

Butch was living out Micah 6:8—doing right, loving kindness, and walking humbly before his God. And his lifestyle was making an impact on that certain teammate, now turned friend. When both men were selected to attend the Arizona Instructional League to prepare for the major leagues, his friend asked if he could room with him. "Out there [in Arizona] I quizzed him more and more," he recalls.

How could this be? What about that? Explain this. Answer that. He was patient, and he was consistent. His answers always came from the Bible.[2]

Eventually, the flame that Butch was carrying so steadily started warming his friend's soul, and one night in the small hotel room in Arizona that friend gave his heart to Christ.

Butch's friend went on to the big leagues and became a World Series Most Valuable Player and star pitcher for the Los Angeles Dodgers. His name? Orel Hershiser. Butch, however, had already made it to Christ's major league of all-star torchbearers—which after all, is God's favorite team.

Butch's story illustrates what it means to write your own chapter of the book of Acts. In what ways can you live out Micah 6:8 before your friends and pass on the torch of Christ?

_____

_____

_____

1. Orel Hershiser with Jerry B. Jenkins, *Out of the Blue* (New York, N.Y.: Jove Books, 1990), p. 79.

2. Hershiser, Jenkins, *Out of the Blue*, p. 80.

Living Insights

Before we place the book of Acts back on the shelf, let's leaf through it one last time. We've divided the book into three major sections:

- The Church Established at Jerusalem (chaps. 1–7)
- The Church Scattered to Judea and Samaria (chaps. 9–12)
- The Church Extended to "Remotest Part" (chaps. 13–28)[3]

Take a moment to thumb through the first section of Acts, using your Bible or previous study guide.[4] Look for one or two events in this section that are the most meaningful to you. As you write them down, what insights do you glean from them? How can you apply these insights to your life?

Events: _____

_____

_____

Insights: _____

_____

_____

Applications: _____

_____

_____

Now do the same for the second section of Acts.

Events: _____

_____

---

3. See the chart titled "Acts: The Spreading Flame" at the beginning of this study guide.

4. You can obtain our first two study guides, *The Birth of an Exciting Vision* and *The Growth of an Expanding Mission*, by writing to Insight for Living, Post Office Box 69000, Anaheim, California 92817-0900.

Insights: _____

_____

_____

Applications: _____

_____

_____

    And the third.

Events: _____

_____

_____

Insights: _____

_____

_____

Applications: _____

_____

_____

    Now share what you've learned from Acts with someone, and spread a little of Christ's flame throughout your world today.

BOOKS FOR
PROBING FURTHER

O ne rich dividend of having studied the book of Acts is the new life it can breathe into your understanding of the apostles' letters. For instance, when you read Peter's words about "a living hope" (1 Pet. 1:3), you'll be able to feel the passion he felt when thousands turned to Christ's light after his preaching, when the lame man jumped to his feet at his touch, when the angel led him from his prison cell to freedom. Or think of Paul's words, "For to me, to live is Christ, and to die is gain" (Phil. 1:21). Can't you sense his commitment to Christ—a commitment carved out by the turbulent rivers of persecution and sacrifice?

We hope this kind of vitalizing study of Acts will spread to your study of the rest of the New Testament and bring new excitement to your soul. If you would like to delve deeper into the truths the apostles have taught us, we've isolated some topics from this study guide and used them to compile the following list of resources. May the insights they provide add to your understanding of the apostles and enliven your study of Scripture.

Commentaries on the Book of Acts

Harrison, Everett F. *Interpreting Acts: The Expanding Church.* Grand Rapids, Mich.: Zondervan Publishing House, Academie Books, 1986.

Kistemaker, Simon J. *Exposition of the Acts of the Apostles.* New Testament Commentary series. Grand Rapids, Mich.: Baker Book House, 1990.

Marshall, I. Howard. *The Acts of the Apostles.* Tyndale New Testament commentaries. Grand Rapids, Mich.: William B. Eerdmans Publishing Co., 1980.

Studies of the Life of Paul

Meyer, F. B. *Paul: A Servant of Jesus Christ.* Fort Washington, Pa.: Christian Literature Crusade, 1988.

Pollock, John. *The Apostle: A Life of Paul*. Wheaton, Ill.: Scripture Press Publications, Victor Books, 1985.

The Church

Anderson, Leith. *A Church for the 21st Century*. Minneapolis, Minn.: Bethany House Publishers, 1992.

————. *Dying for Change*. Minneapolis, Minn.: Bethany House Publishers, 1990.

Colson, Charles, with Ellen Santilli Vaughn. *The Body: Being Light in Darkness*. Dallas, Tex.: Word Publishing, 1992.

Hull, Bill. *The Disciple Making Church*. Old Tappan, N.J.: Fleming H. Revell Co., 1990.

Wilkins, Michael J. *Following the Master: Discipleship in the Steps of Jesus*. Grand Rapids, Mich.: HarperCollins Publishers, Zondervan Publishing House, 1992.

Defending Christianity

Brown, Steve. *If Jesus Has Come*. Grand Rapids, Mich.: Baker Book House, Raven's Ridge Books, 1992.

Erickson, Millard J. *Does It Matter What I Believe?* Grand Rapids, Mich.: Baker Book House, 1992.

McCallum, Dennis. *Christianity: The Faith That Makes Sense*. Wheaton, Ill.: Tyndale House Publishers, Living Books, 1992.

Sproul, R. C. *Essential Truths of the Christian Faith*. Wheaton, Ill.: Tyndale House Publishers, 1992.

Weston, Paul. *My Problem with Christianity Is . . .* Wheaton, Ill.: Harold Shaw Publishers, 1992. Originally titled *Why We Can't Believe*.

Adversity and Stress

Alcorn, Randy and Nanci. *Women under Stress: Preserving Your Sanity*. Portland, Oreg.: Multnomah Press, 1986.

Minirth, Frank, et al. *The Stress Factor*. Chicago, Ill.: Northfield Publishing, 1992.

Stanley, Charles. *How to Handle Adversity*. Nashville, Tenn.: Thomas Nelson Publishers, Oliver-Nelson Books, 1989.

Swenson, Richard A. *Margin: How to Create the Emotional, Physical, Financial, and Time Reserves You Need*. Colorado Springs, Colo.: NavPress, 1992.

Tada, Joni Eareckson. *Glorious Intruder: God's Presence in Life's Chaos*. Portland, Oreg.: Multnomah Press, 1989.

Spiritual Disciplines and Inner Healing

Augsburger, Myron S. *The Christ-Shaped Conscience*. Wheaton, Ill.: Scripture Press Publications, Victor Books, 1990.

Beers, V. Gilbert. *Turn Your Hurts into Healing*. Old Tappan, N.J.: Fleming H. Revell Co., 1988.

Seamands, David A. *Healing Grace*. Wheaton, Ill.: Scripture Press Publications, Victor Books, 1988.

Whitney, Donald S. *Spiritual Disciplines for the Christian Life*. Colorado Springs, Colo.: NavPress, 1991.

Charismatic Issues

Babcox, Neil. *A Search for Charismatic Reality: One Man's Pilgrimage*. Portland, Oreg.: Multnomah Press, 1985.

Some of the books listed here may be out of print and available only through a library. All of these works are recommended reading only. With the exception of books by Charles R. Swindoll, none of them are available through Insight for Living. If you wish to obtain some of these suggested readings, please contact your local Christian bookstore.

ACKNOWLEDGMENTS

I nsight for Living is grateful to the source below for permission to use their material.

Life Application® Bible. Wheaton, Ill.: Tyndale House Publishers, 1991. Maps © 1986, 1988 by Tyndale House Publishers, Inc. Maps are listed according to *The Strength of an Exacting Passion* page number; *Life Application Bible* page numbers have been provided for reference.

Page 4: Ministry in Ephesus and End of the Second Journey (*Life*, p. 1997).

Page 13: Paul Takes a Third Journey (*Life*, p. 2000).

Page 46: Through Macedonia and Achaia (*Life*, p. 2003).

Page 55: Paul Travels from Troas to Miletus (*Life*, p. 2004).

Page 65: Paul Returns to Jerusalem (*Life*, p. 2007).

Page 102: Imprisonment in Caesarea (*Life*, p. 2011).

Page 136: The Trip toward Rome (*Life*, p. 2020).

Page 153: Paul Arrives in Rome (*Life*, p. 2021).

Life Application is a trademark of Tyndale House Publishers, Inc., Wheaton, Illinois, 60189. Used by permission. All rights reserved.

ORDERING INFORMATION

Cassette Tapes and Study Guide

This Bible study guide was designed to be used independently or in conjunction with the broadcast of Chuck Swindoll's taped messages on the topic listed below. If you would like to order cassette tapes or further copies of this study guide, please see the information given below and the Order Forms provided at the end of this guide.

THE STRENGTH OF AN EXACTING PASSION

As you come to the close of most books, you find the story winding down—knotty conflicts untangle themselves, loose ends reconnect, and adventurers return home. The book of Acts, however, is an exception.

Instead of slowing to a satisfying stop, the concluding chapters continually pick up speed. The driving force is the apostle Paul and his white-hot passion to reach Rome with the gospel of Jesus Christ. Nothing can stop him: not a frenzied riot, a murder plot, a shipwreck, or chains. His is the strength of an exacting passion—a passion that can be yours as well, as you come alongside him and let his zeal—God's zeal—ignite your soul.

So join us, won't you, for the passionate and exciting final chapters of Acts!

			Calif.*	U.S.	B.C.*	Canada*
SEP	CS	Cassette series, includes album cover	$73.47	$68.50	$84.00	$79.80
SEP	1–10	Individual cassettes, includes messages A and B	6.76	6.30	7.61	7.23
SEP	SG	Study guide	5.31	4.95	6.37	6.37

*These prices already include the following charges: for delivery in **California**, applicable sales tax; **Canada**, 7% GST and 7% postage and handling (on tapes only); **British Columbia**, 7% GST, 6% British Columbia sales tax (on tapes only), and 7% postage and handling (on tapes only). **The prices are subject to change without notice.**

SEP	1-A:	*Discipleship on Display*—Acts 18:18–21, 24–28
	B:	*The Magnificence of Insignificance*—Acts 18:18–23; 19:1, 7
SEP	2-A:	*Are Tongues and Prophecy for Today?*—Acts 19:1–7
	B:	*God's Extraordinary Power*—Acts 19:8–20
SEP	3-A:	*Peace in Spite of Panic*—Acts 19:21–41
	B:	*Sailing, Speaking, and Sleeping in Church*—Acts 20:1–12

SEP 4-A: *A Touching Farewell*—Acts 20:13–38
     B: *Man's Advice versus God's Voice*—Acts 21:1–17

SEP 5-A: *When Misunderstanding Takes Control*—Acts 21:17–39
     B: *An Unanswerable Argument*—Acts 21:40–22:30

SEP 6-A: *When Pressure Mounts*—Acts 23:1–23
     B: *Between the Frying Pan and the Fire*—Acts 23:23–24:9

SEP 7-A: *Man's Favorite Excuse*—Acts 24:10–27
     B: *Disciplines That Cultivate Maturity*—Acts 25:1–22

SEP 8-A: *Almost Persuaded . . . but Not Quite*—Acts 25:23–26:32
     B: *How to Enjoy a Shipwreck*—Acts 27

SEP 9-A: *Time to Heal*—Acts 28:1–10
     B: *Chained . . . but Offering Freedom*—Acts 28:11–24

SEP 10-A: *The End of the Beginning*—Acts 28:23–31
     B: *What Pleases God?**—Selected Scripture

*This message was not a part of the original series but is compatible with it.

How to Order by Mail

Simply mark on the order form whether you want the series or individual tapes. Mail the form with your payment to the appropriate address listed below. We will process your order as promptly as we can.

United States: Mail your order to the Listener Services Department at Insight for Living, Post Office Box 69000, Anaheim, California 92817-0900. If you wish your order to be shipped first-class for faster delivery, add 10 percent of the total order amount. Otherwise, please allow four to six weeks for delivery by fourth-class mail. We accept payment by personal check, money order, or credit card. Unfortunately, we are unable to offer invoicing or COD orders.

Canada: Mail your order to Insight for Living Ministries, Post Office Box 2510, Vancouver, British Columbia V6B 3W7. Allow approximately four weeks for delivery. We accept payment by personal check, money order, or credit card. Unfortunately, we are unable to offer invoicing or COD orders.

Australia, New Zealand, or Papua New Guinea: Mail your order to Insight for Living, Inc., GPO Box 2823 EE, Melbourne, Victoria 3001, Australia. Please allow six to ten weeks for delivery by surface mail. If you would like your order sent airmail, the delivery time may be reduced. Using the United States price as a base, add postage costs—surface or airmail— to the amount of your order. Please use the chart that follows to determine correct postage. Due to fluctuating currency rates, we can accept only personal checks made payable in United States funds, international money orders, or credit cards in payment for materials.

Overseas: Other overseas residents should mail their orders to our United States office. Please allow six to ten weeks for delivery by surface mail. If you would like your order sent airmail, the delivery time may be reduced. Using the United States price as a base, add postage costs— surface or airmail—to the amount of your order. Please use the chart that follows to determine correct postage. Due to fluctuating currency rates, we can accept only personal checks made payable in United States funds, international money orders, or credit cards in payment for materials.

Type of Postage	Postage Cost
Surface	10% of total order
Airmail	25% of total order

For Faster Service, Order by Telephone or FAX

For credit card orders, you are welcome to use one of our toll-free numbers between the hours of 7:00 A.M. and 4:30 P.M., Pacific time, Monday through Friday, or our FAX numbers. The numbers to use from anywhere in the United States are **1-800-772-8888** or FAX (714) 575-5049. To order from Canada, call our Vancouver office using **1-800-663-7639** or FAX (604) 596-2975. Vancouver residents, call (604) 596-2910. Australian residents should phone (03) 872-4606. From other international locations, call our Listener Services Department at (714) 575-5000 in the United States.

Our Guarantee

Our cassettes are guaranteed for ninety days against faulty performance or breakage due to a defect in the tape. For best results, please be sure your tape recorder is in good operating condition and is cleaned regularly.

Note: To cover processing and handling, there is a $10 fee for *any* returned check.

Insight for Living Catalog

Request a free copy of the Insight for Living catalog of books, tapes, and study guides by calling **1-800-772-8888** in the United States or **1-800-663-7639** in Canada.

Order Form

SEP CS represents the entire *The Strength of an Exacting Passion* series in a special album cover, while SEP 1–10 are the individual tapes included in the series. SEP SG represents this study guide, should you desire to order additional copies.

Item	Calif.*	Unit Price U.S.	B.C.*	Canada*	Quantity	Amount
SEP CS	$73.47	$68.50	$84.00	$79.80		$
SEP 1	6.76	6.30	7.61	7.23		
SEP 2	6.76	6.30	7.61	7.23		
SEP 3	6.76	6.30	7.61	7.23		
SEP 4	6.76	6.30	7.61	7.23		
SEP 5	6.76	6.30	7.61	7.23		
SEP 6	6.76	6.30	7.61	7.23		
SEP 7	6.76	6.30	7.61	7.23		
SEP 8	6.76	6.30	7.61	7.23		
SEP 9	6.76	6.30	7.61	7.23		
SEP 10	6.76	6.30	7.61	7.23		
SEP SG	5.31	4.95	6.37	6.37		
					Subtotal	
					Overseas Residents *Pay U.S. price plus 10% surface postage or 25% airmail. Also, see "How to Order by Mail."*	
					U.S. First-Class Shipping *For faster delivery, add 10% for postage and handling.*	
					Gift to Insight for Living *Tax-deductible in the United States and Canada.*	
					Total Amount Due *Please do not send cash.*	$

If there is a balance: ☐ Apply it as a donation ☐ Please refund
*These prices already include applicable taxes and shipping costs.

Payment by: ☐ Check or money order payable to Insight for Living ☐ Credit card

(Circle one): Visa MasterCard Discover Card Number_____

Expiration Date_____ Signature_____
We cannot process your credit card purchase without your signature.

Name_____

Address_____

City_____ State/Province_____

Zip/Postal Code_____ Country_____

Telephone (___)_____ Radio Station____ ____ ____ ____
If questions arise concerning your order, we may need to contact you.

Mail this order form to the Listener Services Department at one of these addresses:
Insight for Living, Post Office Box 69000, Anaheim, CA 92817-0900
Insight for Living Ministries, Post Office Box 2510, Vancouver, BC, Canada V6B 3W7
Insight for Living, Inc., GPO Box 2823 EE, Melbourne, VIC 3001, Australia

Order Form

SEP CS represents the entire *The Strength of an Exacting Passion* series in a special album cover, while SEP 1–10 are the individual tapes included in the series. SEP SG represents this study guide, should you desire to order additional copies.

Item	Calif.*	Unit Price U.S.	B.C.*	Canada*	Quantity	Amount
SEP CS	$73.47	$68.50	$84.00	$79.80		$
SEP 1	6.76	6.30	7.61	7.23		
SEP 2	6.76	6.30	7.61	7.23		
SEP 3	6.76	6.30	7.61	7.23		
SEP 4	6.76	6.30	7.61	7.23		
SEP 5	6.76	6.30	7.61	7.23		
SEP 6	6.76	6.30	7.61	7.23		
SEP 7	6.76	6.30	7.61	7.23		
SEP 8	6.76	6.30	7.61	7.23		
SEP 9	6.76	6.30	7.61	7.23		
SEP 10	6.76	6.30	7.61	7.23		
SEP SG	5.31	4.95	6.37	6.37		
					Subtotal	
Overseas Residents Pay U.S. price plus 10% surface postage or 25% airmail. Also, see "How to Order by Mail."						
U.S. First-Class Shipping For faster delivery, add 10% for postage and handling.						
Gift to Insight for Living Tax-deductible in the United States and Canada.						
Total Amount Due Please do not send cash.						$

If there is a balance: ❏ Apply it as a donation ❏ Please refund
*These prices already include applicable taxes and shipping costs.

Payment by: ❏ Check or money order payable to Insight for Living ❏ Credit card

(Circle one): Visa   MasterCard   Discover Card   Number_____

Expiration Date_____   Signature_____

We cannot process your credit card purchase without your signature.

Name_____

Address_____

City_____ State/Province_____

Zip/Postal Code_____ Country_____

Telephone (   )_____ Radio Station____ ____ ____ ____

If questions arise concerning your order, we may need to contact you.

Mail this order form to the Listener Services Department at one of these addresses:
Insight for Living, Post Office Box 69000, Anaheim, CA 92817-0900
Insight for Living Ministries, Post Office Box 2510, Vancouver, BC, Canada V6B 3W7
Insight for Living, Inc., GPO Box 2823 EE, Melbourne, VIC 3001, Australia